Praise for *Divine Dirt*

"With her enchanting storytelling and extensive knowledge, Charity takes us on a mesmerizing journey through the secrets of our planet, both above and below the earth's surface….She guides us in harnessing dirt's energy and shows us how to utilize it in various magical practices such as spellcasting and potion making."

—SHAWN ROBBINS, bestselling coauthor of *Wiccapedia and The Good Witch's Guide*

"Guiding the reader on how to tap into energy in and of a location and how to commune spirits of that location…. Bedell leaves no clump of dirt unexplored. Expect to find new ways to invoke health, healing, luck, and love as well as creative curses and protective wards."

—JUDY ANN NOCK, bestselling author of *The Modern Witchcraft Book of Crystal Magick*

"This is a book I will keep as an heirloom and a source book….There were some things in here that I didn't think I would ever see make it to print. And I have to say it's a job well done…Buy this book. Borrow this book and forget to give it back so someone has to buy another one. I said what I said."

—KENYA COVIAK, host of *My Magical Cottagecore Life* podcast

"A masterpiece showing the importance of magic of place. Engaging and easy-to-understand explanations, spells, and recipes are throughout this wonderful book....Not only does this book cover the magic, spell craft, and rituals involving dirt, it also touches on offerings to spirit and divination."

—**BISHOP SEAN WILDE UE,** author of *Magic Without Tools*

"An accessible and approachable book that gets us back to our roots. Bedell takes something as simple as the dirt beneath our feet, and through her ability to capture reverence, she creates something absolutely magical. This book will help you get back to the undeniably powerful basics of the earth."

—**TONYA A. BROWN,** author of *The Door to Witchcraft*

"You'll hear folk talk about graveyard dirt but how about bank dirt for money spells? Corporate dirt? It's rare that I see these Olde Ways resurrected from the dust. Puns notwithstanding, I found this a fun and informative read."

—**MICHAEL CORRELL** (a.k.a. Uncle Birch)

"Bedell takes the Earth-based religion of Witchcraft back to the ground floor, embracing the powerful magic within the dirt....*Divine Dirt* weaves a profound spell of rich lore and encompasses all the ways that dirt can be used in your magic, whether it's used in spell-crafting, ritual, or connecting to the enigmatic spirit of place."

—**CHRISTIAN DAY,** author of *The Witches' Book of the Dead*

DIVINE
DIRT

Photo provided by HMages:
Photography by HM & Hilareigh Maxson

About the Author

Charity L. Bedell (Maine), also known as Loona Wynd, is one of the coauthors of The Modern-Day Witch series and the Wiccapedia Spell Deck. She has studied conjure with Starr Casas and Feri with Veedub, and she is initiated in the Temple Tradition. Bedell has written for *The Witches' Almanac* and *Kindred Spirit Magazine*, and she has presented at festivals such as WitchCon2020. Learn more at Mystic -Echoes.com.

CHARITY L. BEDELL

DIVINE DIRT

THE ART OF USING DIRT IN MAGIC, RITUAL & SPELLCRAFT

LLEWELLYN PUBLICATIONS
WOODBURY, MINNESOTA

FIRST EDITION
First Printing, 2024

Based on book design by Christine Ha
Book format by Samantha Peterson
Cover design by Shannon McKuhen
Interior art on pages 258, 271 by Llewellyn Art Department

Llewellyn Publications is a registered trademark of Llewellyn Worldwide Ltd.

Library of Congress Cataloging-in-Publication Data (Pending)
ISBN: 978-0-7387-7740-5

Llewellyn Worldwide Ltd. does not participate in, endorse, or have any authority or responsibility concerning private business transactions between our authors and the public.

All mail addressed to the author is forwarded but the publisher cannot, unless specifically instructed by the author, give out an address or phone number.

Any internet references contained in this work are current at publication time, but the publisher cannot guarantee that a specific location will continue to be maintained. Please refer to the publisher's website for links to authors' websites and other sources.

Llewellyn Publications
A Division of Llewellyn Worldwide Ltd.
2143 Wooddale Drive
Woodbury, MN 55125-2989
www.llewellyn.com

Printed in the United States of America

Other Books by Charity L. Bedell

The Good Witch's Guide: A Modern-Day
Wiccapedia of Magickal Ingredients and Spells
(cowritten with Shawn Robbins, Sterling Ethos, 2017)

The Good Witch's Perpetual Planner
(cowritten with Shawn Robbins, Sterling Ethos, 2019)

The Wiccapedia Spell Deck: A Compendium of
100 Spells & Rituals for the Modern-Day Witch
(cowritten with Leanna Greenaway
and Shawn Robbins, Sterling Ethos, 2020)

The Modern-Day Witch 2023
Wheel of the Year 17-Month Planner
(cowritten with Shawn Robbins, Sterling Ethos, 2022)

Container Magic: Spellcraft Using
Sachets, Bottles, Poppets & Jars
(Llewellyn, 2023)

Dedication

This book is dedicated to my father, Daniel Bedell, who taught me to respect the earth and land from a young age. He was the first person to teach me the phrase: "No one messes with Mother Nature," and he was the person who taught me that all life has a spirit, a force, and a life. I would not be the animistic witch I am today if it weren't for him. Thank you for all of the support, Dad. I love you.

Disclaimer

The publisher and author assume no liability for any injuries caused to the reader that may result from the reader's use of content contained in this publication and recommend common sense when contemplating the practices described in the work. In the following pages you will find recommendations for the use of certain essential oils, incense blends, and ritual items. If you are allergic to any items used in the exercises, please refrain from use. Essential oils are potent; use care when handling them. Always dilute essential oils before placing them on your skin, and make sure to do a patch test on your skin before use. There are spells in this text that deal with mental illness support. These spells are to supplement proper treatment for your mental health, and they are not substitutions for treatment by a professional. If you are in crisis, talk to a professional and get proper treatment first. Only use the spells after seeking professional help.

CONTENTS

Introduction ... 1

PART I: THE BASICS
Dirt, Earth & the World around You ... 11
Gathering & Harvesting Dirt ... 25
Ethics, Magic & the Law ... 37

PART II: SPELLS & MAGICAL WORKS
Foot Tracks ... 45
Animal Tracks ... 79
Home & Work ... 123
Natural Locations ... 149
Businesses, Public Services & More ... 189
Social Spaces ... 223
Crossroads ... 255
Cemeteries & Graveyards ... 293

Contents

PART III: RESOURCES

Location Correspondences ... 319

Animal Correspondences ... 323

Herb, Root & Flower Correspondences ... 325

*Crystal, Stone, Mineral & Other Curios
     Correspondences ... 333*

Magical Formulas ... 337

Conclusion ... 349

Acknowledgments ... 351

*Appendix I: Exercises, Rituals & Spells in Order
     of Appearance ... 353*

Appendix II: Exercises, Rituals & Spells by Intent ... 361

Recommended Reading ... 375

Bibliography ... 381

Introduction

It was a sunny summer day and I was out in my yard harvesting some plantain leaf (*Plantago major*) and dandelion root (*Taraxacum officinale*). As I harvested the roots, I noticed a ton of dirt stuck to them. I then remembered a recent lesson I had received from my Conjure teacher about the use of dirt and how you can use the dirt from plants for the same type of magical work. I went inside and grabbed a jar for the plantain leaf, dandelion roots, and the dirt. As I gathered the herbs and dirt, I said prayers and gave offerings to the plant spirits and the spirit of the land for letting me harvest the plants and work with their energy. Years later the dirt was used in healing work to aid my father during recovery from an accident.

A few years ago, a friend of mine approached me for some magical help. There were some women he worked with who were gossiping and causing him trouble. He didn't want to target the women; he wanted something for himself. I crafted him a small charm bag with stop sign dirt and a few other items to protect him from the gossip. He contacted me a few weeks later and told me that the spell worked well, and he was grateful.

One time, when I was closing at the pharmacy store I worked at, a customer came in looking for something to help with their constipation. The pharmacy itself was closed, but the rest of the retail store remained open. I told the customer a few things that had worked for me and been recommended by my doctors for general use. Later that night, my manager told me I should have just shown them the over-the-counter remedies and left it at that. If there was a problem with what I suggested, the store could get into trouble because I was not a certified pharmacist or pharmacy technician. To protect myself and the store from any potential legal ramifications, I gathered up some dirt from the store and used it with stop sign dirt to cast a spell.

Dirt is very powerful, and each of the spells I just mentioned used dirt as a key ingredient. While other spells may have also been effective, the use of specific dirt in those spells provided a direct solution through magical action.

Origins of My Practice

My interest in working with dirt started after a customer at a festival asked me why I didn't have any magical dirt for sale. They made a point; dirt was not something that I had seen anywhere on the market. Shortly thereafter, my Conjure instructor had a special class focused on working with dirt. From that point on, dirt became a large part of my magical practice.

I have been practicing magic and witchcraft in some way, shape, or form since I was thirteen. Ever since my childhood, I have had a relationship with the land. As I practiced witchcraft, I noticed that my relationship with the land became deeper. I would honor the spirits in nature, and I would talk to them as a friend.

When I was growing up, my parents would take me on a lot of hikes, and we spent a lot of time enjoying the wilderness around our small camp, which included mountains, woods, and a small pond. The majority of these excursions were on hidden trails that only hunters knew about. These hikes instilled a sense of awe and wonder for nature within me.

It was in my early teens that I discovered the religions of Witchcraft and Wicca. The practice of honoring the Wheel of the Year and the connection with nature soothed my soul. My parents had raised me to honor and love the earth, and that was something that I did not find within Christianity. Witchcraft and Wicca did have that connection.

As I studied and developed my understanding of Witchcraft, I learned that there were many different styles and traditions. I learned that some were more focused on the spirits of the land than the god and goddess and that others were more focused on working with ancestral spirits alongside the god and goddess.

It was through my exploration of Traditional Witchcraft that I was able to really understand folk magic and the origins of many ritual practices I found within modern Wicca. The practice of ancestor veneration within Traditional Witchcraft made me want to find a way to connect with my ancestors, who may have practiced a form of Catholic folk magic.

While my mother did not raise me Catholic, she did teach me about the saints and how they were prayed to for guidance and assistance. When I asked my ancestors how to best connect with them and their beliefs, the clear message was to look into the magic of the saints. That connection with the saints is what ultimately brought me to Conjure and Hoodoo.

Conjure as a magical tradition was developed by those who were enslaved in order to preserve what they could of their ancestral culture. Once those individuals were no longer enslaved, the practice of Conjure found its way into the general public. This is why my Conjure teacher, Mama Starr Casas, believes that Conjure is open to everyone. She teaches that as long as you respect the ancestors of Conjure (those who were enslaved) and work with those ancestors as well as your own ancestors, you can practice Conjure.

It is with that spirit that I began to practice Conjure works alongside my witchcraft practice.

Contents of this Book

The two systems that make up the majority of my practice are witchcraft and Conjure. In this text you will find a mixture of witchcraft, Conjure, and other folk magic practices. There are some practices I use that come directly from Conjure and others that are inspired more by witchcraft. Since I was taught to use the Bible in Conjure work, any of the spells that are influenced by Conjure or that come from Conjure will have the appropriate Bible verses quoted.

Conjure is capitalized to honor the magical tradition of Conjure and to make a distinction from the practice of conjuring spirits. In general, *witchcraft* will be presented with a lowercase *w* to make a distinction between the magical practice of witchcraft and the religion of Witchcraft.

Measurements and Making It Your Own

This spell book, like others, will have a list of materials for each spell. Some spells will have specific measurements listed (e.g., 2 teaspoons, 1 tablespoon), while other spells may have a measurement of a pinch. These spells come from my own experience, and the measurements are a guideline only. Start with the measurements given first, and then adjust as your intuition guides you. It is important to make this magic your own.

Ethics

Within this text you will find that there are spells for helping other people. These spells always require consent. Sometimes you may be asked to cast spells on behalf of another person. In this case, you still need to have the consent of the person who will be impacted by the magical work. If there is no consent, you are imposing your will on others, and that is unethical.

As this is a spell book based on a variety of traditions, you will find baneful magic in this text. You must use your own ethical judgment when reading about or using these spells. I personally follow a path and practice where casting baneful magic is not only allowed but encouraged if the situation calls for it. Your path may not hold the same beliefs.

Even if you decide to not engage in baneful magic, understanding how and why an item is used in such magic can deepen your understanding of the material. Additionally, if you understand the uses of baneful magic, you will better be able to protect yourself against it.

Why Dirt

Dirt is something that can be found everywhere. No matter where you go on this planet, you will be able to find dirt in some shape or form. This magical ingredient doesn't require much preparation. Dirt is easy to use and find, and it can be a very versatile tool when working your magic.

Working with dirt will help you develop a deeper connection with the world around you, and this book will help you on that path.

How this Book Is Organized

This book begins with an introduction to the basics of working with magical dirt, including the tools, tips, and tricks needed to begin your journey. The second part of the book focuses on the actual work at hand. At the end of this text, you will find resources, including correspondences and formulas. Within the spells, rituals, and exercises, you will often find measurements for herbal ingredients. Unless the spell specifies fresh herbs, all herbs used in this book are dried and ground. The general rule of thumb is to work with what you have available, and dried herbs can typically be found year-round these days.

I highly recommended that you have a notebook at your side as you read through this text. I have included several exercises that you will want to record your experiences from. These exercises build on each other and help you grow and develop your skills and abilities as a witch or magical worker. You will also want to perform some of these exercises multiple times. Having a single notebook to record your experiences in will help you compare one experience to another and see the similarities and differences.

It is my hope that by the end of this book you will not only look at dirt differently but be able to see how magic is all around you every day. You just need to be creative and learn to tap into it. Good luck and welcome to the magic of dirt.

PART I
THE BASICS

Dirt, Earth & the World around You

Magical dirt is a topic that needs more attention than it gets. Open any magical book and you can find information on herbs, crystals, and the occasional animal part. Dirt is hardly ever mentioned, and when it is, it's typically cemetery or crossroads dirt. There are so many other types of dirt a person can work with; it is time that magical dirt got the attention it deserves.

The element of earth has many magical qualities, and one of them is the ability to transform energy. This is why many magical practices involve sending energy into the earth after work is performed. Excess energy can be absorbed by the earth and used for its own needs. The same concept applies to burying objects in the earth for twenty-four hours to cleanse them.

The Energy of Dirt

When you work with dirt, you are working with the energy of the location or place it was gathered from. The energy of any location is made up of everything that is there, including all the plants and any animals living there. Any activity or action that takes place there will also flavor the energy.

Before you can begin to work with the energy of a place, you need to be able to sense it. Once you learn to sense the energy of different locations, you can begin to develop your own magical correspondences with them.

Keep in mind that we all have preconceptions about locations and the energy within. Take a look at your beliefs about a variety of locations, both urban and natural. You can do this by simply making a list of locations and writing down what you associate with each of them. These personal thoughts and associations are key to working with the energy of those locations.

SENSING THE ENERGY OF PLACE

This exercise will teach you how to sense the energy of any place you visit. In public locations, perform this exercise when there are as few people around as possible. This will give you the best results; the energy from people in public locations can alter how a place feels. You can try this exercise in public at different times (busy, empty, morning, night, etc.) and notice the differences.

MATERIALS
- Pen
- Notebook or some paper

WORKING

1. Begin by choosing two different locations, such as your bedroom and the grocery store. The locations do not matter as long as you can easily get there and be alone for a bit to do this exercise.

2. Go to one of the two locations and find a place where you will not be disturbed for a few minutes. Once you've found your spot, take a few deep breaths to calm and center yourself. Focus on what you are about to do. One way to do this is to inhale for four counts, hold for four counts, and exhale for four counts before starting again. Repeat this breathing exercise four times for a total of five sets.

3. Sit or stand comfortably. Place your hand out, as if you are about to receive something. With your other hand, use the index and middle fingers together to direct the energy from the ground up your leg, through your chest, and down into your palm. As the energy enters your palm, begin to shape it into a small ball. When you feel that it has become a substantial energy ball, stop directing the energy and let what has started to flow finish in the ball.

4. Hold the energy ball in both of your hands. As you hold the ball, focus on what you feel. Take note of any specific words, thoughts, images, or sensations that occur. When you can no longer comfortably hold on to the energy ball, place your hands palms down on the floor or ground and push the energy back into the earth.

5. Once you're done grounding the excess energy, stand up and wipe your hands to cut the energy transfer.

6. Using the pen, write down everything that you remember from your experience in your notebook. I recommend repeating the exercise in the same location several times, keeping track of similarities and differences.

7. Go to the second location and repeat steps 2 through 6.

8. Look over the notes for both locations and examine the similarities and differences.

9. Repeat steps 1 through 6 as you wish for any and all locations you go to regularly. Repeat the same steps for the locations you listed when examining your preconceptions. Make a note of what locations felt the same as you thought and which ones felt differently. Whenever you repeat the exercise, refer back to your notes. Document the differences and experiences each time. This is how you will build your personal correspondence to these locations.

ALIGNING YOUR BODY & ENERGY WITH THE LOCATION

Another way to sense the energy of a location is to channel its energy into your body and align the energy of your body with it.

MATERIALS
- Pen
- Notebook or some paper

WORKING
1. Begin by choosing two different locations. You can choose any two locations you like. They just have to be two different places.

2. Go to one of the two locations and find a place where you will not be disturbed for a few minutes. Once you've found your spot, take a few deep breaths to calm and center yourself. Focus on what you are about to do. One way to do this is to inhale for four counts, hold for four counts, and exhale for four counts before starting again. Repeat this breathing exercise four times for a total of five sets.

3. Once you are centered, stand with your legs naturally and comfortably positioned. Take a breath. As you inhale, feel the energy of the location entering your body through one foot and exiting your body through the other foot. Exhale and take another breath. With this inhale, the energy will move further into your body,

15

traveling through your foot, up your ankle, calf, thigh, hip, into and through your core, through your arm and up your neck, through the crown, and back down the other side. With your third breath, the energy of the location will flow completely through you and back to the ground, creating a loop.

4. Once the energy is cycling through your body, focus on how it feels as it flows through you. Notice any images, feelings, and sensations you have.

5. Continue the process until you reach your twelfth breath. When you take your twelfth breath, raise your foot to cut off the energy input and force the rest of the location's energy out of your body. Take a moment and ground. Place your foot back down and walk around to shake off any excess energy remaining in your body. Begin to feel your body's energy returning to normal.

6. Use the pen to record your experience with this exercise in your notebook.

7. Go to the second location you selected and repeat steps 2 through 6.

8. Look over what you wrote and make note of the similarities and differences. Repeat the exercise as you wish for any and all locations that you visit regularly.

Genius Loci—The Spirit and Power of Place

All the energy you sense at a location comes from one force. This force is the spirit of the location, or the genius loci. When you bring the energy of a location into yourself, you bring the essence of the spirit into you as well. The energy that you bring into yourself is slightly charged by your energy, allowing the spirit to get a sense of your energy.

The genius loci is made up of multiple spiritual and energetic forces; all of the life forces in the area come together to create the genius loci. The genius loci then looks after and protects that area from harm. In urban locations, such as malls, airports, and medical buildings, it's not just the energy of the beings that live there that give life to the genius loci but the energy of the actions and work being done.

Every location is going to have its own spirit, and each spirit will have its own personality. As spirit and energy workers, it is essential that we get to know each spirit on a personal level. These relationships create magic and provide us with the power to create change in our lives. In his book *Working Conjure*, Hoodoo Sen Moise explains it quite well when he says: "The spirit of place is something that folks need to begin to feel out, in order to understand its potential."[1] Building relationships with spirits takes time and work but is well worth the effort in the end. The stronger your relationship with the spirit of the location is, the stronger the magic you will be able to work.

Communicating with Spirits

There are many ways to develop relationships with the spirits of locations. The simplest method is to spend time with them. Developing a relationship with a spirit does not have to involve elaborate formal rituals. You can develop relationships with spirits simply by talking to them and giving them gifts or offerings.

COMMUNICATE WITH THE SPIRIT OF PLACE

This exercise provides a simple way for you to develop relationships with the spirits of the land. When a building is built on land, the spirit of that land's energy can be found in its foundation and floors.

You will want to repeat this exercise once a month until you can just sense the spirit and can speak to them without the meditative state. After developing a sense for the spirit of the land your home is on, try this exercise at some of the other

---

1. Moise, *Working Conjure*, 87.

locations you have been doing work with. As always, record and make note of all your experiences.

MATERIALS
- Pen
- Notebook or paper

WORKING
1. Find a place in your home where you will not be disturbed for a few minutes. When you find your spot, take a few deep breaths to calm and center yourself. Focus on what you are about to do. One way to do this is to inhale for four counts, hold for four counts, and exhale for four counts before starting again. Repeat this breathing exercise four times for a total of five sets.

2. Get yourself seated comfortably. With your next exhale, state:

    I am here to meet with the spirit of this location. I wish to develop a relationship with you.

3. Close your eyes and relax. Just be at one in the moment and focus on the spirit of the location. Take a mental note of any images and sensations you have when you focus on the spirit.

4. When you can no longer comfortably sit in this light meditative state, thank the spirit for their time. Open your eyes and stand up.

5. With the pen, write down everything you experienced.

Making Offerings to Spirit

Alongside the meditative exercise, you can also give offerings to spirits. These offerings are not payment for work but a symbol of your desire to develop a partnership with them and work with them. Different spirits have different tastes when it comes to offerings. The only real universal offering is fresh water (spring water is preferable, but any clean, fresh water will work).

Milk and honey are two common offerings for spirits. The essence of both milk and honey nourishes them. Other food offerings such as freshly baked bread, fruits, and veggies can be left out on a plate for the spirit to eat. If the offering is eaten by the local wildlife, that's perfectly acceptable, as the animals are directly connected to the spirit of the land. Just be sure that any food offerings you give are safe for the local wildlife.

Personal effects are also offerings that can be given. Personal effects include things such as hair and nails, as well as clothing or other items owned by the individual. Hair is one of the most common offerings, but items like a piece of your favorite shirt or a scrap of fabric from a plushie that means a lot to you are also acceptable. The personal effect just needs to be meaningful to you; you are offering the spirit something of yourself. Just be selective about which spirits you give an offering of a personal effect to. In my own practice, those offerings go to my ancestors and the spirit of the land I live on.

The only way to find out for sure what the spirits will take is to give them offerings. As you give different offerings to more spirits, you will begin to get a feel for what each spirit likes, and eventually you may end up finding out what their favorite offerings are. You can then use those offerings when asking for help and thanking them for it.

Spirits will let you know if an offering is not acceptable to them. Sometimes a message of dislike will come in the form of bad luck or poor sleep with upsetting dreams. Other times you may get a sensation of disapproval from the spirit. When I am in doubt about an offering, I use a pendulum and do a quick yes/no divination. If the answer is yes, I go ahead and give the offering. If the answer is no, I find other possible offerings and continue using the pendulum until one gets yes as an answer.

Another way you can honor land spirits is to donate to local wildlife charities and nature preserves. Let the spirits know that you are giving this money in their honor and name. They will appreciate the donation. The better preserved the land can be, the happier the spirits will be and the more wildlife you will find in those locations.

Make an Offering
to a Land Spirit

This exercise will get you into the practice of giving offerings to spirits, and the goal is to just get you started developing a relationship with the spirits of the land. After a while, you may find that the spirits have different ways they want to be contacted and certain offerings they want to be given.

MATERIALS
- Shot glass or small cup
- Small amount of honey
- Paper
- Pen

WORKING
1. Go to your chosen location and find a place where you will not be disturbed for a few minutes. When you find your spot, take a few deep breaths to calm and center yourself. Focus on what you are about to do. One way to do this is to inhale for four counts, hold for four counts, and exhale for four counts before starting again. Repeat this breathing exercise four times for a total of five sets.

2. If you are outside, working directly with the earth, use your hands to dig a small hole in the ground. It just needs to be deep enough for you to place your offering of honey and cover it. If you are inside your home or another location,

place the shot glass or small cup somewhere it won't be disturbed or seen by other people.

3. Pour the honey into the hole or the container. As you pour, state that it is a gift to the spirits and a sign of your friendship with them.

4. If you dug a hole, fill it in with the dirt. If you are using a glass or cup, make sure it is hidden. It should look like there is nothing out of the ordinary.

5. Stand up and stay still for a moment. Notice any feelings you have as you stay by the offering for a moment.

6. Once you've left your offering, record your experiences in your notebook. Update the entry as you notice how the spirits respond to the offering.

Gathering & Harvesting Dirt

Now that we have covered building relationships with the spirits of the land and various locations, it is time to start talking about the actual practice of gathering dirt. Some locations will be easier to harvest from and work with than others.

Assessing the Location

When you go to gather dirt, there are several things that you need to consider. The first is whether the chosen location is public or private.

If a location is privately owned, you must get permission from the owner to be there. Being on private property without permission is trespassing and illegal. Always make sure you have permission to be on private property.

Public locations often have hours of operation. It is during these times that people are allowed to be there and use the land. Gathering dirt from these locations after hours is another form of trespassing. When you need to gather dirt from a public place (be it a park or business), always consider the hours of operation as part of your preparation. There are other legal and ethical considerations as well, and these are covered in the chapter "Ethics, Magic & the Law."

Other than time of day, it is important to find a spot where you will not be disturbed. Harvesting dirt from a location is a magical act—an act that connects with the spiritual world. When you harvest dirt for your magical work, you want to make sure you will be free from distractions and can focus entirely on the connection between you and the spirit of the location. When visiting the location, take mental notes of places that are out of sight and where you are not likely to be disturbed.

Preparation and Spirit Permission

When harvesting dirt, the first thing that needs to be done is to ask the spirit for their permission. It's a simple sign of respect. Often before asking for permission, a small offering is given. This first offering is a general offering. It is a symbol of your relationship with the spirit and your desire to work with them.

Part of asking permission is telling the spirit what work you plan to do with the dirt. For best results, tell the spirit what you are gathering the dirt for and why you need it. The closer the spirit's energy aligns with the work, the more effective the dirt will be in your spellcraft.

If the spirit answers no, then you need to respect that decision and leave. When the spirit says yes and provides permission, you can then use your tools and gather what dirt you need. Keep in mind that you only need a small bit of dirt for magic to be effective.

The best way to ask the spirit for permission is with a form of yes/no divination. Flipping coins or using pendulums works especially well for this. I prefer using pendulums as they allow for a maybe answer, which then gives me an opportunity to talk to the spirit about what I am doing and why. The method of divination doesn't matter, though, as long as you can get a clear yes or no answer. Use whatever methods work best for you.

Tools of the Trade

One of the reasons working with dirt magically can be so easy is that there are very few tools needed to be successful, and the tools are really only used to gather and store the dirt. The following list is made up of tools that I use in my practice and recommend. You are free to use the tools that work best for you.

Trowels

Trowels are great for digging into and moving small areas of earth, making them excellent tools when burying items or gathering dirt. When you use a trowel for gathering dirt, it's less like digging and more like scraping a little dirt to the side. You will only use this tool in natural locations, such as outside your home, cemeteries, places with stop signs, and at crossroads.

Feathers

Feathers can be used to dust dirt off objects and to create small piles to harvest from. Note that feathers from many birds are illegal to own, and feathers found in nature can be full of bacteria. If you wish to use a feather, buy it from an ethical source or use chicken feathers processed and harvested directly from a farm.

Miniature Brooms

Miniature brooms are great little tools. They can be used to cleanse an area energetically before you harvest dirt, and they can also be used to gather small piles of dirt. Simply use the broom to physically sweep the area, directing the dirt into a pile.

Plastic Baggies

When harvesting dirt, you can put the soil in plastic baggies. These baggies can easily fit in your pockets or purse compartments, letting you carry them with you anywhere. You may want to have a marker or other such utensil to label the baggies, especially if you gather dirt from multiple locations at once.

Storage Containers

Small glass jars, tins, or bottles are a key tool to invest in. Small containers are fine, as you don't need a lot of dirt for the magic to work. Be sure to label each container so you know what magical dirt you have available.

Gathering Dirt

When you gather dirt for magical work, you only need to gather what you can get with a single sweep of your chosen tool or hands. You do not need to go digging deep. It will take a while to build up a collection of dirt, and it may be easier to just gather dirt as you need it.

Gathering dirt at natural locations is easy. You just need to find an area where you can discreetly leave an offering and gather the dirt. Once the dirt is collected, you can then leave payment and return home.

Public locations such as libraries, banks, or hospitals are a little trickier. One option is to gather the dirt outside the building. Many public locations will have plants growing in a garden or something like a garden. These are great places to discreetly harvest dirt from. Not only will the dirt contain the essence of the place but it will also contain the essence of any plants growing there.

The second option for urban locations is to use dirt found in doorways. Doorways will always have some lingering dirt—no matter how well the place is cleaned. Dirt from doorways also has the benefit of opening or closing pathways based on whatever work you are doing. Any dirt that you gather from a doorway can be used in road opening spellwork. Doors allow access to what lies behind them. This means that dirt from doorways has the energy of allowing or denying access to specific energy. Doorway dirt can be used in spells to help open the path or to close the path depending on the spell at hand.

The key to gathering dirt is to be casual and have your plastic baggies on hand and ready to receive dirt. When I have needed to gather dirt but haven't had a baggie with me, I used spare tissues I had on hand instead. I then transferred the dirt to a container when I got home. As long as you have a way to carry the dirt so it is not loose in your pockets or bag, it does not matter what you use.

Paying the Coin

The last part of harvesting and gathering dirt is the payment for the dirt. Like humans, spirits enjoy being compensated for their time and effort. When you harvest dirt, the spirits are giving you a small piece of them, and the offering you leave once you're done is payment for it. Payment for the dirt can be in the form of an actual coin. This practice is called paying the coin. After all, one way to ensure that something is yours and belongs to you is to pay for it. In *A Grimoire for Modern Cunning Folk* Peter Paddon wrote, "By paying the coin, the leader becomes—temporarily—sovereign over the Land, and is able to take possession of it fully."[2] Once you've paid the coin, you have ownership over the dirt and can use it as you see fit.

GATHERING DIRT & PAYING THE COIN

This exercise will get you out and gathering dirt to work with magically.

MATERIALS
- Form of yes/no divination
- Water offerings
- Plastic baggie
- Coin

WORKING
1. Choose one of the locations you have been working with to gather dirt from and go there. Find a spot where you can be alone, and give your first general offering. Do this as you would any other time.

---

2. Paddon, *A Grimoire for Modern Cunning Folk*, 58.

2. Talk to the spirit and let them know why you need the dirt. Use your chosen form of divination to ask them if you can gather some dirt.

3. If the answer is no, then leave the offering of water and come back another time. If the answer is yes, quietly and discreetly gather some dirt in your baggie.

4. Once you have gathered the dirt you need, place the coin where you gathered the dirt as payment.

5. With the dirt paid for and offerings made, return home and label the dirt with the name of the location you gathered it from.

Formal Rituals

Formal rituals can be useful when working with new spirits or gathering dirt from a place you have traveled a significant distance to reach. As always, it is still important to remember to ask the spirit's permission before taking the dirt. When the answer is no, continue the ritual with your offerings and thank the spirit for their time.

A RITUAL TO HARVEST DIRT

The structure and tool use of this ritual is influenced by the religion of modern eclectic Wicca. Any sacred device or tool that is pointed is an appropriate substitute for a wand or athame. If needed, you can simply use your index and middle fingers on your dominant hand to focus and direct the energy. The hair needed for this ritual can be taken from your hairbrush. If hair is not an option, you can use fingernail clippings or even your own saliva. You can find the recipe for spirit offering incense in part 3.

MATERIALS
- Lighter or matches
- Candle
- Candleholder
- Spirit offering incense
- Censer
- Charcoal disc
- Feather or miniature broom
- Bowl of water
- Wand or athame
- Honey, wine, or fresh water
- Coin
- A few strands of your hair
- Empty jar with lid

WORKING
1. Once you've found an appropriate spot at your chosen location, set all your tools on the ground or on a small stump or rock that can act as your temporary ritual altar.

2. Place the candle in its holder and the charcoal disc in the censer. Use the lighter or matches to light the candle and charcoal. Once the charcoal is smoking, add a few pinches of incense.

3. Starting in the north, take your feather or broom and begin walking in a clockwise fashion, creating a circular perimeter around the area where you will be gathering dirt. This area will become your sacred ritual space. As you walk the circle, use the feather or broom to dust the negativity and unwanted energy out of the area. Trace the ritual circle three times with your tool, removing the negative energy and making sure there is no unwanted or negative energy left in the area. As you brush away the negativity, chant:

   I cleanse this space today. Sacred energy blesses and stays.

4. With the unwanted energy removed, start directing energy from the sun and the sky down your arm, out the feather or broom, and into the ground. Trace the perimeter of the ritual area once more. This time direct the energy from the sky and the earth around the circle. As you walk the circle this time, state:

   By the powers of earth and sky this space is blessed.

5. Starting in the north again, sprinkle water from the bowl around the ritual circle with the broom or feather. Continue sprinkling water and traversing the ritual area three times once more. As you sprinkle the water, chant:

   Water, cleanse and clean. Remove the negative, which is unseen.

6. Place the bowl of water and the broom or feather on the ground or temporary altar. Pick up your wand or athame and walk the ritual circle, using the tool to send out a silver or white glowing wall of energy, sealing the area.

7. When you return to the north starting point, stamp the ground three times with your feet. State:

   The circle has been cast around. Now the realm of spirit can be found.

8. Now that the circle has been cast, you can start the work of honoring the spirit and gathering the dirt. Raise the container of honey, wine, or water. Hold it over your head and state:

   I offer this to you, spirit of the land. That I honor you and honor the connection between us.

9. Dig a hole using your hands or a tool at the base of a tree or sturdy plant and pour the offering of honey, wine, or water into the ground and bury it.

10. Now state what your work is. Tell the spirit of the land what you want to use the dirt for.

11. Take your empty container and begin to gather the dirt. Only gather what you need and leave no trace of your actions. As you gather the dirt, feel the energy pulsing in the container.

12. When you have gathered enough dirt, seal the container tight with its lid. As you do so, know

that the energy is being sealed in the container. Use your wand or athame to draw a pentacle over the container. Set the wand or athame on the ground or temporary altar. Place the container on the ground.

13. Go to another tree or sturdy plant, dig another hole, and place the coin and your hair inside it. State:

     Thank you for the power you lend to me.
     For thanks, blessed shall you be.

14. Cover up the coin and your hair with the dirt from the hole. Sit there with the spirit in the circle for a bit longer. If you have more honey, wine, or water with you, take the time to share it with the spirit.

15. Point your athame at the ground and begin tracing the circle back. Trace the circle three times, drawing the energy from the earth into your athame or wand.

16. After completing the third circle, point your wand or athame to the sky and release all of the energy into the sky. State:

     The circle has been released. The veil has
     been closed and reality returns to normal.

17. Pick up your altar supplies and walk away, returning to your home.

Ethics, Magic & the Law

Before we get into the work, there's one more concept we need to discuss: ethics and legalities. Working with dirt requires you to not only consider your ethics but the ethics of the spirits you work with as well. You also need to know and follow the laws regarding land in your area.

Working with Spirits

Asking a spirit to do work that they are against is not only unethical but an abuse of your relationship. While spiritual beings are allies, friends, and helpers in magical and spiritual work, they have their own desires, wants, and needs. They are not beings or tools that we can command at our will. Always ask a spirit's permission before including them in your spellwork. Having a spirit consent to working with you is an essential part of effective magic. If a spirit says no, respect that answer. Working with dirt that was taken without the consent of a spirit is essentially the same as trying to control that spirit.

Don't Trespass

There are social and legal considerations when doing this work, and you need to consider the actual locations themselves. Businesses and other such locations have hours of operation. Only harvest dirt during those hours. Gathering dirt outside of business hours could be considered trespassing.

Is the property private? When you harvest materials from private property and you have not been invited, or have no reason to be there, you are trespassing. When you need to gather dirt that is on private property, ask for the owner's permission. If you can't get their permission, you must find a different spot.

Environmental Impact & Protected Land

When it comes to natural locations, you need to consider the environmental impact of gathering dirt and harvesting materials. There are many insects that live in dirt, and the bacteria and other microorganisms within dirt often provide food and nutrients to plants and animals that live in the area. Removing dirt from these locations can disturb the circle of life, and you must make sure to leave minimal impact. The goal is to leave the location with it looking as if you were never there.

Offerings that you leave need to be nature friendly, such as foods (breads, fruit, veggies, etc.), water, or natural, unsweetened juices. These foods provide an energetic offering and nourishment for the creatures that live within those regions.

Before you harvest dirt from a natural location, check your local laws regarding the land. You want to make sure that you are not taking dirt from protected lands. Protected lands, like the dunes along Maine's coastline and reserves like the Parker River National Wildlife Refuge in Massachusetts, are areas where it is illegal for humans to walk about freely. In these protected locations, people are only allowed on the trails or boardwalks. They cannot take anything natural from these locations, including dirt.

Magic & Consent

As a practitioner of magic, it can be tempting to cast spells that you believe will be beneficial for the people that you love and care about without their knowledge or consent. This is not a good idea and is frowned against. Whenever you are casting a beneficial spell on or for someone, you must have their consent. By casting a spell without their consent, you are imposing your will upon them. No one likes to have their will overruled by the will of another person.

In addition to opposing your will, it is impossible to know exactly what a person wants in their life. They might not want help dealing with their situation. If they do ask you for help, then you can do work for them, but only do what they are asking—no more or no less. This goes for beneficial spells as well as binding spells and baneful magic. If the person does not want you to cast a spell to bind or harm an individual, don't do it. It's simply a matter of respect.

When it comes to love magic, consent is even more important, and you should never target a specific individual when working a love spell. If you target another person, you are interfering with their freewill and their life. Besides, love spells that target a specific individual can go bad quickly. You could end up being harassed or with a stalker. And if a relationship does develop, you will never know if the relationship is based on real emotions or on your manipulation of the target's emotions. Targeting an individual is just inviting a bad situation. When casting a spell to find love, focus on the type of person (interests, behaviors, etc.) you want, not a specific individual. That way you are not forcing anyone to do anything. You may find that what you get is better than what you imagined.

Baneful Magic

The last area of ethics that I need to cover is baneful magic. An important detail to remember is that baneful magic is not necessarily evil or bad. That which can heal can also harm. Baneful magic is no different. Going forward, both beneficial and baneful workings will be shared. My own personal ethics require me to use all tools at my disposal to protect and defend my loved ones. You must make your own choice.

Before any baneful magic actions are taken, I ask myself a series of questions. If any of the answers are no, maybe, or uncertain, I will not take the magical action. Working magic with uncertainty gets unexpected and uncertain results.

Ethical Questions

The following questions are ones that I use to determine whether baneful magic is a solution to my problem. Before performing any baneful magic, ask yourself the following questions:

- Is there any action or behavior you or your loved one has done that could have inadvertently caused jealousy, or other negative emotions, and led to the behaviors/actions you want stopped?

    If the answer is yes, go no further. Address the base behavior issue (jealousy, frustration, etc.)

from the target first, then you can go forward from there.

- Are there any additional problems or situations in the background that may be causing these behaviors and actions you want stopped?

    If you do not know the answer to this, then take some time and get to know the person behind the situation. Sometimes there are factors beyond an individual's control causing them to act out.

- Have you tried every other method—magical and mundane—to deal with the situation?

    Baneful magic should be the last resort. Before casting a hex or curse, try other magical works to fix the situation; there may be ways to address and fix the situation. Once you have tried all other approaches, you can reevaluate the use of baneful magic.

- Can you live with the consequences of the actions you are about to take?

    This is the big question. To prevent spells from backfiring on you, make sure you are 100 percent certain you can accept all consequences associated with the magical work you are considering.

PART II
SPELLS &
MAGICAL WORKS

FOOT TRACKS

Dirt roads can provide a powerful and interesting tool when it comes to magic and witchcraft. When you walk on a dirt road, you leave a footprint. The dirt taken from these footprints can be used in magic as a personal effect.

Personal effects are items that either connect directly to your target (e.g., strands of hair or fingernail clippings) or is something that they have owned or worn (e.g., old clothing). Effects are powerful, as they contain a person's energy. Foot track dirt is a very subtle personal effect that can be gathered without people knowing. Tayannah Lee McQuillar writes in *Rootwork* that using foot track dirt as a personal effect is "a direct extension of the West African belief that a person's energy can be captured in the tracks they leave behind."[3]

When working with foot track dirt, you need to be careful and make sure the footprints you work from are the footprints of your target. If the foot track dirt belongs to someone else, the magic you work will impact that individual rather than your target.

Protection Magic

When we work magic, we catch the attention of people and spirits, which we may need protection from. Other times, we need protection for and during our daily lives. Sometimes we need protection from something magical in nature, and other times the protection is needed when traveling. The most effective protection magic involves the use of a personal effect. Here are some protection spells that work with foot track dirt.

PROTECTION FROM A DISTANCE POPPET

This is a protection spell that works over long distances. For those who have family or loved ones that travel a lot, this spell is a great way to provide magical protection for them wherever they go.

---

3. McQuillar, *Rootwork*, 44.

MATERIALS
- Small package of air-dry clay
- 3 pinches target's foot track dirt
- 2 teaspoons (10 ml) powdered dragon's blood (*Dracaena cinnabari*) (for protection)
- 7 rose thorns (*Rosa*) (for protection)

WORKING
1. Knead the clay, mixing in the foot track dirt and dragon's blood powder. While kneading the clay, think about the person you want to protect. Direct that energy into the clay.

2. Once the powder and dirt have been thoroughly mixed into the clay, begin to mold and form the clay into a human shape.

3. Once the figure is formed, exhale over it. State:

   Doll of clay, protect (target's name) forward from this day.

4. Place the thorns one at a time in the clay, inserting one thorn in the crown (top of head), one in each arm, one in each leg, and two in the center. As you place each thorn, state:

   Thorn from the rose flower, provide protection for (target's name) in this hour. Keep harm away with your power.

5. Let the clay figure sit and dry. In 24 hours, the clay should be hardened. Once it has, place the clay figure somewhere it won't be disturbed. As long as the figure is intact and safe, your loved one will have extra protection. When you feel

they no longer need it, break up the figure and dispose of the clay and thorns by burying them. If burial isn't possible, respectfully toss the materials into the trash.

NEUTRALIZE BANEFUL ENERGY SPELL

Protecting against negative energy is a very common magical practice. This spell protects your loved one from baneful energy by neutralizing any sent their way. Neutralized energy can't harm anyone. The spell also reverses any energy that could not be neutralized.

MATERIALS
- Small plate
- About ¼ cup (60 ml) sea salt (to neutralize)
- Wand or small stick
- 3 pinches target's foot track dirt
- 1 teaspoon (5 ml) ground black peppercorn (*Piper nigrum*) (for protection, removal, reversal)
- Miniature broom

WORKING
1. On the plate, pour out the sea salt. You want to use enough salt to cover the plate in a thin, even layer. As you place the salt on the plate, state:

   Salt from the sea, neutralize all negativity.

2. Use the tip of the wand or stick to draw a human figure in the salt. As you do so, state the name of the individual you are neutralizing the energy for.

3. Sprinkle the target's foot track dirt in the center of the figure. State:

   Foot track dirt from (target's name), let this salt neutralize unwanted energy sent to (target's name).

4. Sprinkle the ground peppercorn around the figure. As you sprinkle it, state:

   Black peppercorn that is ground, turn that which cannot be neutralized right back around where the source can be found.

5. Use the miniature broom to carefully brush over the human shape, visualizing any baneful energy being neutralized.

6. Brush the figure one more time, directing the materials into the trash. Know that all unwanted energy is now gone.

PROTECTION ON THE GO CHARM

This spell is for when you are traveling away from home and want to make sure your loved ones are safe while you are away. This spell works best when gone on short-term trips (no more than 7 nights).

MATERIALS
- Small glass vial
- 1 teaspoon (5 ml) foot track dirt from each individual you wish to protect
- ½ teaspoon (2.5 ml) powdered dragon's blood (for protection)
- ½ teaspoon (2.5 ml) angelica root (for protection)

- ½ teaspoon (2.5 ml) ginger (for protection)
- Necklace chain

WORKING

1. Place the dirt and each herbal material into the small vial one at a time. As you add each herbal material, state:

   To protect (name) while I'm away.

2. Seal the vial with its topper.

3. Shake the vial to mix the materials. As you shake the vial, repeat the following chant five to seven times:

   Protection for (name) today. All my love and protection sent to them while I'm away.

4. Attach the vial to the chain. You can now either wear the vial and have it hang close to your heart or carry it with you while traveling.

Healing with Foot Track Dirt

An excellent way to use foot track dirt is in healing magic. Healing magic is my specialty. Here are some fun and easy healing spells that use foot track dirt. These spells are variations on my favorite healing spells.

HEAL THY WOUNDS POPPET SPELL

This spell is focused on healing mental, emotional, and physical wounds.

MATERIALS

- Pen
- 2-by-4-inch or 4-by-4-inch (5-by-10-cm or 10-by-10-cm) piece of blue fabric
- Scissors
- Pinch of target's foot track dirt
- 2 teaspoons (10 ml) ground coriander seeds (*Coriandrum sativum*) (for healing)
- 2 teaspoons (10 ml) ground lemon zest (*Citrus × limon*) (for protection, cleansing, removal)
- 2 teaspoons (10 ml) lemon balm (*Melissa officinalis*) (for healing)
- Small bowl
- Spoon or wand
- Pin or needle

WORKING

1. Use the pen to draw a human shape on the fabric.

2. Use the scissors to cut the shape from the fabric. Dispose of the remaining fabric.

3. Set the human shape in the center of your workspace. Use the pen to mark the locations of the wounds that need healing.

4. Add the dirt, seeds, and herbs to the bowl, and use the spoon or wand to mix them together. As you stir, think about what needs to heal. Once the mixture has been mixed thoroughly, set the bowl beside the fabric figure.

5. Pick up the human figure. Exhale one breath over it to give it life. Name it for the individual who needs healing.

6. Apply the herbal mixture like a paste to the marked areas that need healing. As you tend to each spot, state:

> **Take this wound from (target's name) today. With the wounds healed, (target's name) can now play.**

7. Use the pin or needle to stab through the areas that have been covered by the mixture. As you stab each point, state:

> **From (wound), (target's name) is free.**

8. Set the figure and remaining herbal mixture in a place where they will not be disturbed. Once a week, repeat steps 6 and 7 until the wounds have healed or the issues have cleared up. Make more of the herbal mixture as needed. When your target's wounds have healed to their satisfaction, toss the fabric figure and any remaining mixture into the trash.

WELLNESS BOOST POWDER SPELL

This spell brings good health and wellness into a person's life with each step they take. For best results, have access to the shoes of the individual who needs the boost. When access to the target's shoes isn't available or practical, you can use a personal effect or image of them and 18-inch (45-cm) doll shoes instead. The recipe for wellness boost powder can be found in part 3.

MATERIALS
- Small bowl
- 2 tablespoons (30 ml) wellness boost powder
- 3 teaspoons (15 ml) target's foot track dirt
- Spoon or wand
- Shoes of the individual receiving the boost or personal effect or image and doll shoes

WORKING
1. In the bowl, combine the wellness boost powder with the foot track dirt, stirring them together with the spoon or wand. As you mix, chant the following three times:

    A boost of wellness for (target's name).

2. Sprinkle the powder under their shoe lining. If shoe linings are not available, sprinkle a little of the powder across the bottom of their shoes. As you sprinkle, state:

    Each step they take this day brings health and wellness their way.

3. If you're using a personal effect or image instead of the target's shoes, place it on your work surface along with the doll shoes. Fill the doll shoes with the dirt and powder mixture. Then, using your hands, walk the doll shoes over the personal effect or image. As you do so, state:

    By the steps these shoes take on this day, wellness is sent (target's name)'s way.

4. Repeat step 2 daily, creating more of the powder as needed, until the wellness boost is no longer required. If you used a personal effect or image, dispose of it in the trash along with any remaining powder mixture.

MENTAL HEALTH AID CANDLE SPELL

The goal of this spell is to provide someone with a little relief when they're going through a rough spot. Note that it will not cure any of the issues.

MATERIALS
- Small plate
- 2 tablespoons (30 ml) target's foot track dirt
- White votive candle
- Pin, needle, or knife
- Candleholder
- 5 blue chime candles
- 5 chime candleholders
- 1 tablespoon (15 ml) lavender (*Lavandula angustifolia*) (for anxiety relief, healing, mood elevating)
- 1 tablespoon (15 ml) chamomile (*Matricaria recutita*) (for anxiety relief, healing, mood elevating, stress relief)
- 1 tablespoon (15 ml) marigold (*Calendula officinalis*) (for healing)
- Lighter or matches

WORKING

1. Clear an area on a shelf or table that you can use for a few days for this magical work.

2. Set the plate in the center of the chosen area, and place the dirt in the center of the plate. As you add it, state:

   Dirt from the tracks of (target's name),
   I ask you today to use your connection to
   (target's name) to send healing their way.

3. On one side of the votive candle, use the pin, needle, or knife to carve your target's name. On the other side, carve "Mental Health Healing."

4. Set the candleholder on top of the dirt and place the votive candle in it.

5. Place the chime candleholders on the plate and around the dirt so that each one makes the point of a star. Place the chime candles in them.

6. Sprinkle the lavender flowers to draw the lines of a pentacle, connecting the candle star points. As you sprinkle the lavender, state:

   For peace of mind and healing.

7. Repeat step 6 with the chamomile and marigold, saying the same statement.

8. Light all the candles, starting with the white votive candle.

9. Once the candles have been lit, state:

   Candles burning bright, to (target's name)
   send your healing light.

10. Let the chime candles burn out. Once they have, carefully extinguish the votive candle.

11. Burn the votive candle for 5 minutes a day until it has completely burned. Once it has, you can dispose of the materials in a trash can near the target's home.

Prosperity, Money & Success

Money spells are among the most commonly requested spells. Here is a collection of prosperity, money, and success spells that work with foot track dirt.

SWEETEN SUCCESSFUL MONEY CANDLE SPELL

Use this spell to bring yourself more success, which, in turn, will bring you more money.

MATERIALS
- Small bowl
- 2 teaspoons (10 ml) of your own foot track dirt
- 1 tablespoon (15 ml) ground apple peels (*Malus domestica*) (for money, wealth)
- 1 teaspoon (5 ml) sugar (for attraction, success)
- 1 teaspoon (5 ml) cinnamon (*Cinnamomum verum*) (for money, success)
- Spoon or wand
- Small plate
- One-, two-, or five-dollar bill
- Green votive candle

- Votive candleholder
- Pin, needle, or knife
- Lighter or matches

WORKING

1. In the bowl, combine the dirt, apple peels, sugar, and cinnamon. Use the spoon or wand to mix well. As you stir, think about your luck, your success, and the money you have earned. When the mixture is well combined, set the bowl down and to the side.

2. Place the small plate in your workspace, and set the money across the center.

3. Gently set the candleholder on top of the cash.

4. Use the pin, needle, or knife to carve the words "Sweet Success" into the candle. Set the carved candle in the candleholder.

5. Sprinkle the herbal mixture around the candleholder, over the bill, and on the plate. As you do so, state:

   Money flowing generously, brings sweet success freely.

   Repeat the statement until all of the mixture has been sprinkled around the candle and covers the cash.

6. Light the candle, stating:

   Candle fire, manifest my desire.

7. Let the candle burn down completely, allowing the wax to drip and do what it wants. If you cannot burn the entire candle in one sitting, burn the candle for 5 to 10 minutes once a day until it has burned completely. Repeat the statement from step 6 each time the candle is lit.

8. Once the candle has burned completely, put away the candleholder. Fold the cash and keep it in your wallet. Clean and wash the plate, disposing of the wax and herbal mixture in the trash respectfully. The cash in your wallet will bring more money and success to you.

Fast Cash Bowl Working

Use this spell to attract cash to you quickly. This spell can be used during emergencies or just when you really need a little extra money. You can find the recipe for fast-money powder in part 3.

MATERIALS
- Large firesafe ceramic bowl
- 2 pinches of your own foot track dirt
- ¼ cup (60 ml) fast-money powder
- Spoon or wand
- Chime candleholder
- Green or gold chime candle
- 2 magnets (for attraction)
- Lighter or matches

WORKING

1. In the bowl, mix the foot track dirt with the fast-money powder, using the spoon or wand to combine the materials. As you stir, repeat the following chant five to seven times:

    Cash comes speedily, cash flows freely.

2. Set the candleholder in the center of the bowl.

3. Place the magnets on opposite sides of the candleholder so they are attracted to each other.

4. Place the candle in the holder, and use the lighter or matches to light it. As you do so, state:

    As this candle burns brightly, money and cash flow to me speedily.

5. Let the candle burn completely.

6. Set the bowl aside as is. Anytime you need a boost in cash, repeat steps 4 and 5.

LUCK GAIN

Sometimes a person goes through a difficult stretch, and they just need a boost of luck to get things going their way again. If someone you know needs help in this department, use this spell to bring good into their life.

MATERIALS
- Small bowl
- Spoon or wand
- 2 tablespoons (30 ml) target's foot track dirt

- 1 tablespoon (15 ml) clover (*Trifolium repens*) (for good luck)
- 1 tablespoon (15 ml) basil (*Ocimum basilicum*) (for good luck)
- 1 tablespoon (15 ml) cinnamon (*Cinnamomum verum*) (for good luck)
- 1 tablespoon (15 ml) sugar (for attraction)
- Small rabbit's foot key chain (as a symbol of luck)
- Skeleton key (to open the way)
- 5 drops pine essential oil (*Pinus*) (for good luck)
- 5 drops clove essential oil (*Syzygium aromaticum*) (for good luck)

WORKING

1. In the small bowl, use the spoon or wand to stir the dirt, clover, basil, cinnamon, and sugar together. While you mix, recite the following mantra five to seven times or until thoroughly mixed:

   > *Lucky day today. Send luck (target's name)'s way.*

2. Anoint the rabbit's foot key chain and the skeleton key with the pine and clove essential oils.

3. Place the key and the key chain in the bowl. Roll both items around until they're covered in the mixture.

4. Place the skeleton key on the rabbit's foot key chain. Hold the charm in your hand and feel an aura of good luck pulsating from it.

5. Give the charm to your friend the next time you see them, and know that you have just opened the way for them to have much better luck.

Love Spells

As a secondary personal effect, foot track dirt has a less direct connection to the target, which makes it an excellent ingredient to use in love magic. The weaker connection ensures that if something does go wrong with the spell, the damage will not be as severe.

A reminder that love spells are best when performed for yourself. You only really know the needs and desires you have for a relationship. It is hard to know for certain what someone else might want.

TRUE LOVE'S LIGHT CANDLE SPELL

Use this spell to bring love into your life.

MATERIALS
- Large plate
- Taper candleholder
- Pin, needle, or knife
- Red taper candle
- 2 tablespoons (30 ml) of your own foot track dirt
- 1 teaspoon (5 ml) cardamom (*Elettaria cardamomum*) (for love, lust)
- 1 teaspoon (5 ml) clover (*Trifolium repens*) (for love)

- 4 dried raspberries (*Rubus idaeus* var. *strigosus*) (for love)
- Lighter or matches

WORKING

1. Set the plate in the middle of your workspace, and place the candleholder on the center of the plate.

2. Carefully use the pin, needle, or knife to carve the words "True Love" into the candle on two sides.

3. Place the candle in the holder.

4. Sprinkle the foot track dirt around the base of the candleholder. As you lay down the dirt, state:

   Foot track dirt of (name), on this day, bring true love here to stay.

5. Sprinkle the cardamom around the candleholder, letting it rest on top of the dirt. As you add it, state:

   A love that's new, a love that's true, a love who will see all things through.

6. Sprinkle the clover on top of the cardamom. As you do so, state:

   Plant that is considered a weed, plant true love's deep seed.

7. Lay the four raspberries in the four cardinal directions. As you place each one, state:

   Berry that is both sweet and sour, bless me with love with your power.

8. Light the candle. State:

   As this candle does burn down, so shall a true love be found.

9. Let the candle burn for 10 to 15 minutes, then extinguish the candle.

10. Once daily, until the candle has burned down completely, repeat steps 8 and 9. When the candle has burned completely, it is time to dispose of the materials. Thank the materials, then place them gently in the trash.

Partners & Lovers Spell

Use this spell to attract a love who will be a true partner to you; it focuses on what is important in a lasting relationship and helps bring that to your life.

MATERIALS
- Large plate
- 2 magnets
- 2 candleholders
- 2 red human-shaped candles (one to represent you and the other to represent the one you're looking for)
- 1 pinch of your own foot track dirt
- 2 teaspoons (10 ml) catnip (*Nepeta cataria*) (for friendship, love)
- 2 sprigs of rosemary (*Salvia rosmarinus*) (for communication, love, opening minds)
- 2 teaspoons (10 ml) damiana leaf (*Turnera diffusa*) (for desire, love, lust)

- Matches or lighter
- 2 to 4 feet (61 to 122 cm) red ribbon

WORKING

1. Set the plate in the middle of your work area. Place the two magnets in the center of the plate. On either side of the plate, place the candleholders. Position one candle in each holder.

2. Sprinkle your foot track dirt over both magnets. As you sprinkle the dirt, state:

   Foot tracks of mine, bring to me a love that is divine.

3. Sprinkle the catnip over both magnets. As you sprinkle the catnip, state:

   A partner and true friend, who will love me till the end.

4. Place a sprig of rosemary on each magnet. As you place each sprig, state:

   For a partner who will communicate with me and be open to my ideas.

5. Sprinkle some damiana leaf over both magnets. As you sprinkle the herb, state:

   For lust based in love and true desire. For lust powered by passion and love.

6. Light one of the candles and state:

   As this candle does burn, true love do I earn.

7. Light the second candle and state:

   By this candle's romantic glow, a true love I shall know.

8. Place the magnets together so all of the herbs are sandwiched between the two magnets.

9. Wrap the red ribbon around the magnets. As you bind the magnets, repeat the following chant:

   A love that's new and true, a partner to see the hard times through.

10. Once the magnets are covered, tie a knot to seal the ribbon around them. Leave the magnet bundle where it is.

11. Let the candles burn for another 5 to 10 minutes. After that time, extinguish the candles.

12. Once a day, until they have burned out completely, light the candles for 5 to 10 minutes, reciting the same two statements used when the candles were originally lit.

13. Once the candles have burned out, you can dispose of them by respectfully tossing them in the trash.

14. Place the magnet charm somewhere you will see it often and it will not be disturbed. Leave the charm there until love manifests, rubbing the charm for love and luck before you go on a date or an outing where you could meet someone.

15. When a relationship manifests, you can cut the ribbon from the magnets and dispose of the

materials. The herbs should be buried in the earth if possible. If that is not possible, respectfully toss the herbs into the trash. The magnets can be cleansed and used in future magical workings.

Friends & Family

When it comes to dealing with interpersonal relationships, there are going to be times when things are tough. Foot track dirt can be a useful aid in spells designed to keep the peace between people. Before working any of these spells, make sure the people are open to your workings. If you work the spells without their consent, instead of bringing peace, the spells will destroy the peace between all parties.

GOOD VIBES—A HAPPINESS & PEACE SPELL

One of the most important things for a healthy and happy life is a peaceful home. In Conjure and witchcraft, it is quite common to find charms that are used to bring peace and calm into the home— and keep it there. This charm does just that; it invokes happiness, peace, and a content life. When gathering the materials, be sure to keep the foot track dirt in separate piles, one for each family member.

MATERIALS

- Slip of paper
- Pen
- Hollow plastic ornament ball with removeable top
- 2 tablespoons (30 ml) of foot track dirt from everyone in the home
- 2 tablespoons (30 ml) marigold (*Calendula officinalis*) (for hope)
- 2 tablespoons (30 ml) lavender (*Lavandula angustifolia*) (for peace)
- 2 tablespoons (30 ml) chamomile (*Matricaria recutita*) (for peace)
- 2 tablespoons (30 ml) catnip (*Nepeta cataria*) (for happiness)
- 2 tablespoons (30 ml) sugar (to sweeten disposition)
- 1 tablespoon (15 ml) amethyst chips (for peace, protection)
- 1 tablespoon (15 ml) sodalite or lapis lazuli chips (for ease of communication, peace in the home)
- Superglue
- Taper or votive candleholder

WORKING

1. On the slip of paper, use the pen to write out "Peace in the Home." Slide the paper into the ornament ball.

2. Add the foot track dirt to the ornament ball. As you add the dirt for each person, state:

   Peace and happiness for (person's name).

3. Add the herbs and sugar to the ornament ball one at a time. As you add each one, state why it is being called on for the working.

4. Add all of the crystal chips to the ball. As you add them, state:

   For a peaceful home.

5. Trace the inside of the ball topper with superglue, and secure the topper to the ball's opening. Set the ball aside to dry.

6. After letting the glue set for 12 to 24 hours, take the ball in your hands and shake it. As you shake the ball, focus on the energy of a peaceful home. Direct all of that energy into the ball. Imagine all members of the household having a peaceful home.

7. Once you feel that the ball has been shaken enough and all of the materials within are mixed, place the candleholder somewhere in the living room where the ball can rest on it and not be disturbed.

Deepen Friendship Sweetening Jar

During our life we make many friends and acquaintances. Sometimes there are people in our circle of friends that we want to know better than we currently do. This spell will help open doors so the relationship can strengthen and deepen. Only perform this spell if the other individual is also interested in developing a stronger and deeper friendship.

MATERIALS

- Small glass jar
- 2 votive candleholders
- Photo of yourself
- Photo of your friend
- Pen
- Pin, needle, or knife
- 2 pink votive candles
- Lighter or matches
- Rubber band
- 2 tablespoons (30 ml) of your own foot track dirt
- 2 tablespoons (30 ml) of your friend's foot track dirt
- 1 cup (250 ml) sugar (for attraction, sweetening)
- ½ tablespoon (7.5 ml) pink rose petals (*Rosa*) (for friendship, love)
- ½ tablespoon (7.5 ml) catnip (*Nepeta cataria*) (for happiness)
- ½ tablespoon (7.5 ml) passionflower (*Passiflora incarnata*) (for friendship)
- 1 sprig fresh rosemary (*Salvia rosmarinus*) (to open the mind)

WORKING

1. Begin by placing the small jar in the center of your workspace. Place the candleholders on opposite sides of the jar. Set the photos down in front of the jar with the pen nearby.

2. Using the pin, needle, or knife, carve your name into one candle. Carve your friend's name into the other. As you do so, think about the friendship you want to strengthen and the things you would like to do together.

3. Set one candle in each holder and light the candles. As you light them, state:

   Candlelight, burning bright, strengthen this friendship on this night.

4. On the back of each photo, write the name of the individual pictured and their date of birth. If you don't know your friend's date of birth, just write out their name and the relationship you have with them.

5. Place the photos on opposite sides of the jar with the backs of the photos facing the jar. Use the rubber band to bind the photos to the jar. As you secure the photos, state:

   By the rubber band, which binds, a stronger friendship do we find.

6. Pour half of the sugar into the jar, stating:

   As sugar is sweet, two friends do meet.

7. Sprinkle the pink rose petals into the jar, stating:

   Pink roses for friendship's delight, brings with it love sweet and light.

8. Place your hand over the jar's top and gently shake the jar while reciting the previous step's chant.

9. Add the catnip, stating:

   Catnip brings happiness today, brings happiness to stay.

10. Again, place your hand over the jar's top and gently shake the jar while reciting the previous step's chant.

11. Add the passionflower to the jar and state:

    The passionflower within lets our friendship begin.

12. Add both sets of foot track dirt to the jar.

13. Place the sprig of rosemary in the jar and state:

    Rosemary, open the mind today, that friendships new may stay.

14. Pour the remaining sugar into the jar. As you add it, state:

    Sugar attracts friends that have each other's backs.

15. Secure the jar's lid tight. Hold the jar and shake it vigorously. As you shake the jar, recite the following chant three times:

    A friendship old and true now renewed. True friends we shall stay. A friendship not going away.

16. Pass the jar safely over both candle flames three times. As you do so, state:

    The candlelight secures the friendship's might. By this candle's light, this friendship shines bright.

17. Repeat steps 15 and 16 until the candles burn out. Once they have, place the jar on your dresser.

18. Shake the jar twice a day (once in the morning and once in the evening). As you shake, recite the following chant three times:

> *A new friendship today; true friends find their way. A new friendship today; great friends that by your side will stay.*

19. Continue this shaking and chanting process until the friendship you desire manifests. When it does, dispose of the contents in a trash can away from your house, preferably one at a favorite hangout you and your new friend share. If it has been three months and the relationship has not manifested, destroy the jar, dispose of the contents, and find a different target. You can also try the spell again with general friendship in mind.

Baneful Magic

When it comes to baneful magic, foot track dirt is especially helpful. It helps direct magic toward your target.

REMOVE PROBLEMATIC COWORKER POWDER SPELL

Use this spell as a last resort when you need to remove a coworker that causes nothing but problems for you and other employees.

For safety, perform this spell outside. The recipe for protect and removal powder can be found in part 3.

MATERIALS
- Fire extinguisher or bucket of water
- Paper
- Pen
- Firesafe ceramic bowl
- Lighter or matches
- 1 teaspoon (5 ml) target's foot track dirt
- 2 teaspoons (10 ml) protect and removal powder
- Spoon or wand
- Small storage container

WORKING
1. Clear your outdoor workspace of all flammable debris, and make sure the fire extinguisher or bucket of water is prepped and ready to go.

2. On the paper, write out the name of the troublesome coworker. Under their name, write out why you want—and need—them removed from work.

3. Read what you wrote on the paper and place it in the firesafe bowl. Light the paper on fire. As it burns, state:

   From (where you work) may you be gone.

4. Once the paper's ash has cooled, sprinkle the foot track dirt into the bowl. State:

   Track dirt of (target's name), on this day may (target's name) be sent far, far away.

5. Add the protect and removal powder to the bowl.

6. Use the spoon or wand to stir the ash, dirt, and powder together. Once the materials are thoroughly combined, move the mixture to the storage container. Label the container and set it aside.

7. The next time you and your target are working together, wait until they go out on a break. When they do, discreetly sprinkle the mixture along a path they regularly walk. As they walk over the powder, the charm will take effect. You should soon find out they are leaving the job or moving away.

CURSE THY NAME SPELL

This spell is a great way to release anger and frustration at someone who is causing you trouble. It is a variation on a traditional justice work, which involves chewing fresh galangal root and then spitting out the root as the name of the person being cursed is said. Due to the nature of this spell, it must be performed in a private area outside.

MATERIALS
- Stick or twig
- 1 pinch target's foot track dirt
- 1 pinch ground galangal root (*Alpinia galanga*) (for baneful magic, justice work)
- 1 pinch cayenne pepper (*Capsicum annuum*) (for justice, speed)
- Your spit

WORKING

1. Use the stick to write your target's name in the dirt.

2. Sprinkle your target's foot track dirt over their name. State:

   Foot track dirt of (target's name), send this curse to them this day. For the problems they have caused, they shall pay.

3. Sprinkle the ground galangal root over your target's name. State:

   For (target's name), who has caused me trouble.

4. Sprinkle the cayenne pepper over your target's name. State:

   For justice and speed.

5. Say your target's name and spit on their name in the dirt. Make sure as much of your saliva is on the written name as possible.

6. Use your foot to scratch out the name from the dirt. As you scratch, direct all your anger and frustration into the movements. Stomp on what was your target's name one last time and walk away.

REPEL GOOD LUCK CURSE

Use this spell to actively direct good luck away from your target. Any remaining luck will change into bad luck.

MATERIALS
- Small human-shaped toy or other figure to represent your target
- Small plate
- 2 magnets
- 2 tablespoons (30 ml) your target's foot tracks
- 2 tablespoons (30 ml) thyme (*Thymus vulgaris*) (for luck)
- 2 tablespoons (30 ml) mace (*Myristica fragrans*) (for luck)
- 2 tablespoons (30 ml) ground black peppercorn (*Piper nigrum*) (for baneful magic, removal)
- 2 tablespoons (30 ml) nettle leaf (*Urtica dioica*) (for baneful magic, removal)

WORKING
1. Set the figure in the center of the plate. State:

    Figure, I name you (target's name).

2. Place the magnets on opposite sides of the figure. Make sure the magnets are repelling one another.

3. Sprinkle the dirt on each magnet, stating:

    Good luck from (target's name), go away.
    Bad luck for them is welcome to stay.

4. Sprinkle half of the herbs over each pile of dirt, stating:

    Remove the good luck today. Ill luck go
    their way should games they play.

5. For the next five days, move the magnets about an ⅛ inch away from the figure first thing in the

morning. By day five, the magnets should no longer be on the plate.

6. When the magnets are off the plate, the spell is complete. Dispose of the dirt and herbs in the trash. Cleanse the magnets and figure so they can be used in other magical work.

ANIMAL TRACKS

Animal track dirt works the same way that foot track dirt does; just as dirt taken from your foot tracks contains some of your essence, dirt from an animal's tracks will contain some of that animals energy and essence. When you work with animal spirits, you engage with very primal forces. Animal spirits were among the first created. Before humans were around, there were animals.

Before harvesting this kind of dirt, make sure you identify the track accurately, or you may find yourself working with the energy of a different animal. Another important thing to consider is how fresh the tracks are. Fresh tracks can mean the animal is close by. Use caution and be safe; do not disturb any animals.

This chapter contains sections focused on specific animal track dirt; the animals included in this chapter do not make a complete list. There are many more animal tracks that can be used in magical work, and some are listed in the book's resource section. If you discover tracks of an animal that is not listed in this chapter or the animal correspondence list, try to observe the animal in the wild. While you observe the animal, try to connect with its spirit. You can then work solely with your findings and experiences.

Developing Relationships with Animal Spirits

Before you start working with the dirt from an animal's tracks, it is a good idea to have a relationship established with the animal spirit. Animal spirits have their own spiritual realm and ways of communicating. You should contact them in some way before trying to work with them, even if the only thing you do is introduce yourself.

Developing a strong relationship with animal spirits can sometimes take more time and effort than with human or plant spirits. Many animal spirits are cautious and careful around humans. Just be patient and take the time to get to know the spirits. Eventually you will be able to develop a relationship with them.

⦿BSERVE & IDENTIFY WILDLIFE

When it comes to developing a relationship with animal spirits, the first step is to learn about the wildlife in your area. Knowing the animals that live in your region will help you identify the tracks you are likely to come across.

MATERIALS
- Wildlife guidebook for your region
- Binoculars
- Pen
- Notebook

WORKING
1. Go to a local nature preserve, park, or area where you often see wildlife. Find yourself a comfortable spot where you can spend an hour or more of your time.

2. Once you're settled, observe any wildlife. Use the binoculars to help you.

3. When you spot any wildlife, use the guidebook to identify what you are seeing.

4. At the top of a page in your notebook, note your location, the date, and the time. Under that information, record what animals you see. Note how you feel observing them. What thoughts come to your mind?

5. After an hour or so, you can pick up and go home. Repeat steps 1 through 4 at other

locations to get a larger view of the wildlife in your area.

6. Once you have seen some of the animals that live in your area, it's time to get to know them more. Read up on them. You do not need to become an expert; it's enough just to get familiar with them and their habits. Learn what they eat and how they behave. Those elements can really enforce the connection you develop with the spirits.

CONNECT WITH AN ANIMAL SPIRIT

To help connect to animal spirits, you will need small stuffed animals and figurines. Many toy stores and even dollar stores have large bags of toy animals. You simply need to be able to hold the figure with one hand. Holding a physical representation of an animal works as a gateway to that specific spirit.

The more you repeat this exercise, the stronger your relationship with the animal spirit will be. For best results, you may want to use a recording device to record the meditation and play it back. If recording the meditation is not an option, then you should find someone to read it out loud to you. You can find the recipe for meditation incense in part 3.

MATERIALS
- White or brown votive candle
- Candleholder
- Censer

- Heat pad
- Tongs
- Self-lighting charcoal disc
- Long-stemmed lighter
- 2 teaspoons (10 ml) meditation incense
- Soft instrumental music or nature sounds
- Small animal figure
- Pen
- Notebook

WORKING

1. Set the candle in the holder. Place the censer on top of the heat pad. Start the music. Use the tongs to hold the charcoal disc and light it with the long-stemmed lighter. Once the charcoal disc has a soft red glow and sparks have gone across the disc, it is ready. Carefully use the tongs to place the disc in the censer.

2. Sprinkle a little of the incense over the charcoal disc (you want the incense to be smoldering, not on fire). A little goes a long way.

3. Begin by taking four breaths. Use these four breaths to ground and focus on the work at hand. When you are ready, listen to the following meditation.

> *Close your eyes and relax. Take a deep breath and slowly exhale. Slowly begin to count back from thirteen to one, visualizing the numbers as you count down. When you reach one, you are at a gentle and light meditative state.*

Begin to count back from twelve to one, this time without seeing the numbers. Relax and feel yourself enter a deeper meditative state. When you reach one, look around you. In front of you is a doorway or screen. On the other side is the realm of animal spirits. Walk through the doorway or screen. When you walk through, you enter a large field.

As you enter the field, see your animal guide resting there, waiting for you. As you greet them, they beckon you to follow them down a path. You follow them to a door or passageway.

Step through the door or passageway to a large open landscape. It matches the type of land you would find the animal living in reality. As you enter the habit, look around. Somewhere, you should sense a powerful force coming from the animal spirit.

When you sense the animal spirit, slowly approach them. Respectfully stand before the spirit and greet them. Ask them for their guidance in working with them. Bow your head in respect and let them approach.

Listen to any sounds you hear and observe any images or feelings you get when the animal approaches. Once the spirit has told you all they plan to tell you, they will walk away and return to where they came from. They may leave you a small token or item as a symbol of your meeting and relationship. Observe the token. It will always be there for you to use to call on the animal guide when needed.

Follow your guide back to the field. Thank them for their help. Know that they will always be there, waiting to guide you on other travels.

Walk back through the first door, returning to your mind. Begin to count up from one to twelve. When you reach twelve, wiggle your fingers and toes to bring awareness back to your body. Slowly count up from zero to thirteen. When you reach thirteen, notice the screen of your mind disappear; this is a sign that you are returning to your body. Take note of the feelings in your body. Once you open your eyes, you have fully returned to your body.

4. Ground and center by wiggling your fingers and toes to bring your mind and senses back into your body. Then place your hands on the ground and push out any energy or sensations remaining from your meditation experience.

5. Extinguish the candle and incense. Turn off the music and ground and center. Record your experiences in your notebook and return to your day.

Ant Hills

Ant hills can be found nearly everywhere. Many of the mounds look like piles of dirt, and that makes sense! Ant hills are made from dirt that the ants dug from the ground to create the maze that is their home. These hills carry the energy of the ants. By using dirt taken from them, you can work with that energy.

When you gather dirt from an ant hill, only take a pinch. Only taking a pinch or two does not disturb the ant colony. You do not want to disturb the ants. In order to make sure you have enough dirt for your magical working, you may need to harvest from more than one ant hill. An abandoned hill is an excellent place to collect this dirt from. For safety, always wear gloves when harvesting this dirt.

ANT OBSTACLE-BUSTER SPELL

This spell is for when you are working on a project and keep reaching blocks. You solve one problem, then another problem presents itself right away. After performing this spell, you should notice that the blocks are gone and there are fewer problems.

MATERIALS
- 2 tablespoons (30 ml) ant hill dirt (for block busting, door opening, perseverance)
- Small bowl
- 3 ground bay leaves (*Laurus nobilis*) (for door opening)
- 1 tablespoon (15 ml) ground black peppercorn (*Piper nigrum*) (for banishment, protection, removal)
- 1 teaspoon (5 ml) cayenne pepper (*Capsicum annuum*) (for protection, speed)
- Spoon or wand

- Skeleton key
- Key ring
- Small plastic container to store the mixture, optional

WORKING

1. Place the ant hill dirt in the bowl. As you add it, state:

   Spirits of the ant, I ask of you, give me the strength to through my blocks bust.

2. Add the bay leaves to the bowl. State:

   Bay leaf to open the door. There shall be troubles no more.

3. Sprinkle the black peppercorn into the bowl. State:

   Black peppercorn, I ask today, protect me from all that would cause me unnecessary delay.

4. Add the cayenne pepper to the mix. State:

   Cayenne pepper, pepper of heat, give me speed to my goals meet.

5. Using the spoon or wand, stir the materials. While you stir, think about the end of your project. Visualize the doors and passageways that lead to your goal being unlocked and opening up. Hold that image for as long as you can, reciting the following chant five to seven times:

   Blocks busted today. Open the roads shall stay. To the goal, opened is the way.

6. When you can no longer hold the image, release the energy down your arms and hands and into the bowl.

7. Bury the skeleton key in the mixture, then hold your hands over the bowl. Visualize the energy of the mixture being absorbed into the key. Feel and direct all of that energy into the key, and recite the following chant three to five times:

   Skeleton key, open the door, take me into the future forever more.

8. Keep the key in the mixture until you feel the key vibrating. You can then place the key onto the key ring.

9. Carry the key with you every day. The mixture can be tossed in the trash or set aside and saved in case you want to charge the charm again. If you want to recharge the charm, repeat steps 6 and 7 once a month until your project has reached completion.

FIRE ANT WALL OF PROTECTION CHARM

This spell uses the energy of fire ants to create a protective barrier around your home. Any negativity or unwanted forces will be escorted away and not allowed to persist.

For safety, gather the dirt from an abandoned hill or where you find dead fire ants. As always, wear gloves.

MATERIALS

- 4 iron nails
- Small bowl
- Olive oil
- 2 pinches dirt from a fire ant hill (for protection, removal, reversal with a sting)
- 1 tablespoon (15 ml) ground black peppercorn (*Piper nigrum*) (for protection, removal, reversal)
- 1 tablespoon (15 ml) cayenne pepper (*Capsicum annuum*) (for protection, removal, reversal)
- 1 tablespoon (15 ml) stinging nettle (*Urtica dioica*) (for protection, removal, reversal)
- Hammer

WORKING

1. Place the iron nails in the bowl and anoint each one with olive oil.

2. Sprinkle the dirt over the nails, stating:

   Ants of fire, protection is my desire.

3. Pour the black peppercorn and cayenne pepper over the nails. As you pour, state:

   Protect me from that which is unwanted and return it to the sender.

4. Add the stinging nettle, covering the nails as much as possible. As you do so, state:

   Protection you bring that comes with a sting.

5. Use your hands to mix all of the materials in the bowl. Your goal is to make sure the nails are as

evenly coated as possible. Be careful as you mix; nails are sharp.

6. Once the nails are coated, go outside and find the most southward-facing wall of your home. Go to the center of that wall. Use the hammer to drive one of the nails into the ground. As you drive in the nail, visualize a wall forming around your home.

7. Repeat step 6 for the other cardinal directions.

8. When the final nail is driven into the ground, see the walls connect and create a cohesive energetic barrier. Know that your home is now protected by it. As long as those nails remain in the ground, your home will be safe.

Bears

When it comes to strength and protection, especially of children, no spirit or force is better than that of the bear. No one messes with a mother bear and her cubs.

Bears also have the power to topple trees and obstacles in their paths. You can use this strength to overcome obstacles in your own life.

When gathering dirt from bear tracks, make sure you know the bear is gone and take proper safety precautions.

Parental Protection Bear Charm

This spell calls on the power of a mother bear to protect a child you care about. It can be your own child or another child you care for.

When gathering the materials for this spell, try to find a medium- to average-sized stuffed bear. If you don't have a seam ripper, you can use a knife or scissors instead.

MATERIALS
- New stuffed animal bear
- Seam ripper
- 1 tablespoon (15 ml) bear track dirt (for protection, strength)
- 3 tablespoons (45 ml) lavender flowers (*Lavandula angustifolia*) (for protection)
- 3 tablespoons (45 ml) angelica root (*Angelica archangelica*) (for protection)
- Thread that matches the stuffed animal's color
- Sewing needle

WORKING
1. Using the seam ripper, remove one of the seams in the back of the stuffed animal.

2. Remove a small portion of the stuffing (only a handful or so) and set it aside.

3. Sprinkle half of the bear track dirt into the stuffed animal. As you add the dirt, say:

   Spirit of a mama bear, I ask you today to protect (child's name) and keep all harm away.

4. Place the lavender flowers inside the bear. As you do so, state:

   Lavender that brings peace and calm, prevent (child's name) from experiencing harm.

5. Sprinkle the angelica root into the stuffed animal. As you add it, state:

   Herb that contains angelic power, I ask you to blast away negativity in this hour.

6. Replace the stuffing you removed earlier.

7. Thread the needle and stitch up the back of the stuffed animal.

8. Rub the remaining dirt into the feet of the stuffed animal. As you rub, state:

   Spirit of the bear, I ask you today to bring protection (child's name) way. Create a shield that keeps ill intent away.

9. Give the stuffed animal to the child as a gift. Let them know it will protect them from harm and keep them safe.

Topple Obstacles Bear Spell

This spell calls on the power of the bear to overcome obstacles in your path. No matter what the obstacles are, know that you have the strength and courage to overcome them.

MATERIALS
- Bear track dirt (to overcome obstacles)
- ½ teaspoon (2.5 ml) basil (*Ocimum basilicum*) (to break blocks)
- 2 to 3 ounces (60 to 90 ml) oven-bake clay
- Pencil or stick
- Red or black acrylic paint
- Paintbrush
- Key ring or necklace chain

WORKING
1. Mix the bear track dirt and basil into the clay. While you mix, focus on overcoming the obstacles in your way.

2. When the elements are thoroughly mixed, make a flat disc with the clay. The clay should be evenly distributed.

3. Use the pencil or stick to draw a bear paw in the clay. Leave room to make a small hole near the top. This will let the disc become a charm of some sort.

4. Hold your hands over the drawing and state:

   Spirit of the bear, I ask you today to help me overcome all obstacles in my way.

5. Use the pencil or stick to make a hole at the top of the disc. You want to make sure the hole is large enough so it won't close while baking.

6. Follow the instructions on the clay's packaging to bake the clay. Once the clay has finished baking, let it cool.

7. Paint the paw red or black, and set the charm aside for 2 hours to dry. Once dry, the charm can be added to the key ring or necklace chain.

8. Carry or wear the finished charm as long as you have obstacles that you need to overcome.

9. When you have overcome all of the obstacles in your path, break the charm. If possible, bury the pieces, returning the energy to the earth. If burial is not possible, find an alternative disposal method, such as gently putting it in the trash. Thank the bear spirit for help.

Cougars

Cougars, pumas, and mountain lions are the same animal. These elegant, powerful cats are one of the largest feline predators in North America. One of the main spiritual and magical associations with these felines is that of adaptability. These cats can live in mountains, deserts, and forests. This wide range of habitats shows that this animal can adapt and survive.

Remember to use caution and common sense when gathering animal track dirt. Only gather dirt from cougar tracks when you know the animal is not around.

STRENGTH TO CHANGE & ADAPT OIL

Change can be overwhelming, and this oil will help you adapt and adjust. Simply anoint yourself and any candles with the oil as needed.

If grape-seed oil isn't available and you're in a pinch, you can use olive oil instead. The infused oil will last for six to nine months if stored in a cool, dark, and dry place.

MATERIALS
- 2 24-oz (710-ml) mason jars with lids
- 2 tablespoons (30 ml) cougar track dirt (for adaptability and strength)
- 2 tablespoons (30 ml) plantain leaf (*Plantago major*) (for strength)
- 5 bay leaves (*Laurus nobilis*) (for strength)
- 2 tablespoons (30 ml) Saint-John's-wort (*Hypericum perforatum*) (for strength and to overcome anxiety and depression)
- 3 sprigs of rosemary (*Salvia rosmarinus*) (for mental focus)
- 2 tablespoons (30 ml) ginkgo leaf (*Ginkgo biloba*) (for mental focus, clarity of mind)
- 2 cups (500 ml) grape-seed oil
- 5 to 7 drops vitamin E oil
- Cheesecloth

- Dropper bottle
- Pen and label stickers

WORKING

1. Place the dirt and all the herbal materials in one of the mason jars. As each item is added, state why you are using it.

2. Add both oils to the same mason jar.

3. Seal the jar, and shake it vigorously for 3 to 5 minutes. While shaking the jar, recite the following chant:

   For strength to adapt and survive, I call upon the cougar to help me thrive.

4. Set the jar in a cool, dark, dry place.

5. Shake the jar two times daily, repeating the same chant from step 3, for the next 4 to 6 weeks.

6. After 4 to 6 weeks, place the cheesecloth over the second jar. Carefully pour the infused oil through the cheesecloth, straining out the herbs, and into the clean jar.

7. Fill the dropper bottle with oil, and label both jars with "Strength to Change and Adapt Oil."

8. To use the oil, simply anoint yourself with two to three drops. You can also anoint any candles used for spells. Use the oil until you are through the changes and hardships.

REFLECT INNER BEAUTY OUTWARD SPELL

Cougars are one of the most beautiful creatures in the world. Their coats and eyes work perfectly as camouflage, and their movements hold the grace of a ballet dancer. Use this spell to call upon their power, boost your self-esteem, and see your true beauty.

MATERIALS
- Mirror with a stand
- Candleholder
- Pin, needle, or knife
- Red or pink chime candle
- 2 pinches cougar track dirt (for beauty)
- Petals from 1 rose (*Rosa*) (for beauty, self-esteem)
- Dried peels from 1 apple (*Malus domestica*) (for beauty)
- 1 tablespoon (15 ml) ginseng (*Panax ginseng*) (for beauty)
- Lighter or matches

WORKING
1. Set the mirror in the center of your workspace, and place the candleholder in front of the mirror.

2. Use the pin, needle, or knife to carve the words "Inner Beauty" into the candle. Place the candle in the holder.

3. Sprinkle the cougar track dirt around the candle, reciting:

   Cougar full of elegance and grace, help me to find true beauty on my face.

4. Lay the rose petals on top of the dirt. As you place each petal, state:

   Beauty within, beauty without, show true beauty with no doubt.

5. Lay the apple peels on top of the rose petals. State:

   Apple, fruit of a flower, enhance my beauty with your power.

6. Sprinkle the ginseng over the apple peels. State:

   Fiery root from deep in the ground, help my true beauty to be found.

7. Light the candle. State:

   By this candle's burning light, true beauty is in my sight.

8. As the candle burns, gaze gently into the mirror. Do so until the candle burns out. While you gaze, notice your inner and natural beauty shining.

9. Dispose of the candle and herbal materials in the trash.

Coyotes

Coyotes are beautiful canines. They are also intelligent and able to blend in with their surroundings incredibly well. It's almost like they disappear within the thickets. For these reasons, coyotes are associated with cunning, luck, wisdom, strength, and trickster spirits.

To Be Cunning in Sales Candle Spell

Being a salesperson is hard work. Perform this spell before your next week of work to enhance your chances of great sales for the week.

MATERIALS
- Large heat-resistant bowl
- Large silver coin
- Chime candleholder
- Gold chime candle
- Pin, needle, or knife
- 2 teaspoons (10 ml) coyote track dirt (to be cunning)
- 2 teaspoons (10 ml) sugar (for attraction, sweetening)
- 1 sprig of rosemary (*Salvia rosmarinus*) (to open the mind)
- ½ teaspoon (2.5 ml) alfalfa (*Medicago sativa*) (for money drawing, prosperity, protection)
- ½ teaspoon (2.5 ml) goldenrod (*Solidago*) (for money)
- Lighter or matches

WORKING

1. Set the bowl in the center of your work area, and place the silver coin in the center of the bowl. Set the candleholder on top of the coin.

2. Use the pin, needle, or knife to carve a "$" into the candle. Set the candle in the holder.

3. Sprinkle the coyote track dirt around the candleholder. As you scatter the dirt, state:

   Spirit of the coyote, cunning and wise, help me to help my customers. Let my sales rise.

4. Sprinkle the sugar around the candle. State:

   Sugar that is sweet, help me to my customers' needs meet.

5. Place the rosemary sprig around the coin. State:

   Rosemary, herb that opens the mind, let my customers listen to me; the items they need I shall find.

6. Sprinkle the alfalfa over the rosemary. As you do so, state:

   Alfalfa, attract customers to which I can sell everything they need to make their life well.

7. Lay the goldenrod down over the alfalfa. As you add it, state:

   Herb with the golden flower, help me make money upon this hour.

8. Light the candle. As the candle burns, state:

   By this candle's gentle glow, great customers shall I know.

9. Let the candle burn out and the wax drip onto the coin.

10. Keep the coin in your wallet. The other materials may be disposed of in the trash.

ATTRACT A LUCKY DAY CHARM

We all need extra luck once in a while, and this charm provides a simple boost. Perform this spell at night so the next day will be full of good luck.

If you cannot find bilberries (*Vaccinium myrtillus*), blackberries (*Rubus*) or raspberries (*Rubus idaeus* var. *strigosus*) can be used as substitutes.

MATERIALS
- Small magnet (for attraction)
- Small plate
- Rabbit's foot key chain (for luck)
- ½ tablespoon (7.5 ml) coyote track dirt (for luck)
- Iron pyrite tumble (for luck)
- 5 dried bilberries (for luck)

WORKING
1. Set the magnet in the center of the plate. As you place the magnet, state:

   Magnet for good luck to attract, and all bad luck send back.

2. Place the rabbit's foot key chain on top of the magnet.

3. Rub the coyote track dirt into the rabbit's foot. State:

> *Coyote, spirit of trickery and luck, with bad luck I'm no longer stuck.*

4. Place the iron pyrite tumble on the key chain. State:

> *Stone of fool's gold, bring good luck as the day does unfold.*

5. Set the bilberries in a star shape around the magnet and rabbit's foot. State:

> *Herb in the shape of a star, bring good luck from near and far.*

6. Leave the plate set up overnight, giving the energy on the plate time to charge the key chain.

7. Carry the charm with you to have a lucky day, and dispose of the bilberries and dirt in the trash. Repeat the spell as needed for lucky days.

Deer

Deer shed and regrow their antlers every year. This action connects deer to death, rebirth, and renewal. Their antlers are also often associated with the rays of the sun. These factors connect deer to the Horned God of many Witchcraft traditions, and dirt from their tracks can be used to work with this deity.

When it comes to traveling through the forest, deer are one of the swiftest animals out there. Their speed allows them to outmaneuver predators like cougars or wolves. Moving swiftly on their hooves, they are able to leap over nearly any obstacle in their path. This same speed can be applied to your magical works by incorporating deer track dirt.

HORNED GOD'S BLESSING

This simple charm allows you to carry some of the essence of the Horned God and his blessings with you at all times. This spell can be performed at any time, but if you are a Wiccan or Witch who follows the Wheel of the Year, you will achieve best results performing it as part of an esbat ritual honoring the Horned God and Goddess of the Moon.

MATERIALS
- Large gold pillar candle
- Candleholder
- Lighter or matches
- Small necklace vial charm
- 2 pinches deer track dirt (to symbolize the Horned God)
- 1 ground and broken acorn top (*Quercus robur*) (for courage, strength and to symbolize the Horned God)
- 3 sunflower seeds (*Helianthus annuus*) (for hope, solar energy, strength and to symbolize the Horned God)
- 18-inch (46-cm) necklace chain

WORKING

1. If performing this spell as part of a sabbat or esbat celebration, set the altar up and perform any ritual preparation as you normally would; otherwise skip to step 3.

2. Begin your ritual and invoke the Horned God and Moon Goddess.

3. Place the candle in its holder on your altar. Place all of the other materials in front of the candle. Light the candle and state:

   Horned God of the woods, lord of the sun, bless these items here with your presence. May they be blessed with your strength and protection that I may carry it with me every day.

4. Sprinkle the deer track dirt into the vial. As you add the dirt, state:

   May power of the stag, animal of the Horned Lord, be present.

5. Add the ground acorn top to the vial. State:

   May the strength of the oak tree be with me.

6. Add the sunflower seeds. State:

   May the blessings of the sun, light, and life be with me this day.

7. Seal the vial and place it on the chain.

8. Carefully pass the vial through the candle flame five times. Each time the vial passes through, the blessing grows stronger.

9. Extinguish the candle and go about your day. If performing this as part of an esbat or sabbat ritual, finish the ritual as you normally would. Wear or carry the charm to keep the blessings of the Horned God with you.

SPEED OF THE DEER HEALING CANDLE SPELL

Use this spell when you need to heal from something quickly. It works for physical healing as well as mental, emotional, and spiritual healing. As with all healing magic, proper medical treatment should be taken before casting the spell.

The recipe for general anointing oil can be found in part 3.

MATERIALS
- Pin, needle, or knife
- Small blue taper or chime candle
- Small bowl
- ¼ teaspoon (1 ml) deer track dirt (for speed)
- ¼ teaspoon (1 ml) lavender (*Lavandula angustifolia*) (for healing)
- ¼ teaspoon (1 ml) allheal (*Prunella vulgaris*) (for healing)
- ¼ teaspoon (1 ml) oregano (*Origanum vulgare*) (for healing)

- ¼ teaspoon (1 ml) coriander (*Coriandrum sativum*) (for healing)
- Spoon or wand
- Healing anointing oil or general anointing oil
- Candleholder
- Lighter or matches

WORKING

1. Use the pin, needle, or knife to carve the words "Speedy Healing" into one side of the candle. On the other side, carve the name of the individual who needs the healing.

2. In the small bowl, mix the dirt and herbal materials together with the spoon or wand. While you stir, chant the following words five to seven times:

   Fast, effective healing.

3. Anoint the candle with the oil, working from top to bottom to remove the ailment causing pain.

4. Gently rub the dirt and herbal mixture on the candle. A small amount should remain in the bowl.

5. Set the candle in the holder, and sprinkle the remaining powder around the base.

6. Light the candle. State:

   As this candle burns bright, speedy healing will set things right.

7. Let the candle burn out. If you cannot burn the candle in one sitting, burn the candle for 10 to 15 minutes a day until it has burned completely.

8. Dispose of the candle by putting it in the trash. If possible, the herbs can be buried or composted. If not, thank the herbs for their help and dispose of them in the trash.

Rabbits

Out of all the animals to work magic with, the rabbit is one of the most well-known. In popular culture, rabbits are seen as symbols of good fortune (think about the lucky rabbit's foot charm) and fertility. Prosperity and abundance are also associated with rabbits. By calling on the power within rabbit track dirt, you can channel those energies into your magical work.

Bring Luck into the Home Spell

Use this spell to bring good luck into your home. A home with good luck is prosperous, successful, healthy, and happy. If bilberries are not available, raspberries or blackberries can be used as substitutes.

MATERIALS
- Horseshoe
- 2 tablespoons (30 ml) rabbit track dirt (for luck)
- 1 teaspoon (5 ml) allspice (*Pimenta dioica*) (to attract luck)

- 1 teaspoon (5 ml) basil (*Ocimum basilicum*) (for good luck)
- ½ teaspoon (2.5 ml) clove (*Syzygium aromaticum*) (for good luck)
- Hanger for the horseshoe
- 6 bilberries (*Vaccinium myrtillus*) (for good luck)
- Iron pyrite tumble (for good luck)

WORKING

1. Lay the horseshoe down on your workspace, and rub the rabbit track dirt into it. As you rub, state:

   Rabbit foot track dirt, in this house luck attract.

2. Sprinkle the allspice, basil, and clove over the horseshoe, asking for luck.

3. Hang the horseshoe on a wall in your living room. It should hang in an upright "U" shape.

4. Place two bilberries on each of the "U" points.

5. Set the iron pyrite in the center of the horseshoe.

6. Place a bilberry on either side of the iron pyrite.

7. Hold your hands over the horseshoe and state:

   Herbs and animal of luck, into the house good luck attract.

8. As long as the horseshoe hangs in your living room, it will attract good luck. To charge the charm, sprinkle a fresh batch of rabbit track dirt or basil, clove, and allspice over the horseshoe once a month.

CONCEPTION AID CHARM BAG

This spell calls on the power of rabbits to aid in the conception of a child. Before casting this spell, make sure there are no medical issues preventing conception and that both parties are on board with having a child.

MATERIALS
- Green drawstring bag
- 3 pinches rabbit track dirt (to aid conception)
- 1 avocado pit (*Persea americana*) (for fertility)
- ¼ cup (60 ml) banana chips (*Musa acuminata*, *Musa balbisiana*) (for fertility)
- Seeds from 1 apple (*Malus domestica*) (for fertility)
- 3 to 5 acorns (*Quercus robur*) (for fertility)

WORKING
1. Place all of the materials in the charm bag. As you add each item, focus on the conception of a child and a safe and healthy pregnancy.

2. Once all of the items are in the bag, seal it.

3. Hold the bag in your hands and play with it, using your hands to mix the materials together. As you do so, call upon the spirit of the rabbit and ask for their help in the conception of a child.

4. Place the charged bag under the mattress where you and your partner sleep and engage in sexual activities. Every time you engage in sexual activity, the charm bag will activate, providing energy for a safe and healthy pregnancy. Once the child

has been born, you may dispose of the bag's contents in the trash. Wash the bag and use it again in other works.

Snakes

Snakes are the subject of many superstitions, and the snake is one of the most common animal spirits associated with magic and witchcraft. In her book *Old Style Conjure*, Mama Starr says:

> *If you are lucky enough to find a snake crossing, scoop up as much dirt as possible. You can work with the dirt for wisdom, protection, knowledge, and enemy works.*[4]

SNAKE BINDING SPELL

Many snakes are constrictors; they don't use venom to kill their prey. Use this spell when you need to bind an enemy and stop their actions. It calls on the energy of constrictor snake spirits.

MATERIALS
- Pen
- 7-by-5-inch (18-by-13-cm) piece of paper
- 3 crushed snail shells (to stop harmful behavior)
- 2 pinches snake track dirt (to bind)
- 1 teaspoon (5 ml) cayenne pepper (*Capsicum annuum*) (for baneful magic)

---

4. Casas, *Old Style Conjure*, 164.

- 1 pinch stinging nettle (*Urtica dioica*) (for baneful magic)
- 18 inches (46 cm) black ribbon
- Scissors

WORKING

1. Write out the name of your target on the paper. If you know their date of birth, write that underneath their name.

2. Sprinkle the snail shells over your target's name. As you sprinkle, state:

   To stop (behavior you want stopped).

3. Sprinkle the snake track dirt over the shells. State:

   By the power of the snake, that constricts and binds, (target's name) is bound. Until (behavior) stops, no relief shall be found.

4. Sprinkle the cayenne pepper and stinging nettle over the paper. State:

   To cause (target's name) to be in pain. In pain they shall remain until (behavior) ceases. Then their freedom shall they gain.

5. Fold the paper in half three times.

6. Wrap the black ribbon around the paper until it is completely covered. While you wrap, chant:

   By the snake's power, you are bound. No harm from you can be found.

7. Once the paper is completely covered, tie a knot.

8. When your target has learned their lesson, use the scissors to cut the ribbon. Toss the packet in the trash to release the spell.

STRENGTH FOR NEW BEGINNINGS SPELL

Sometimes we need a fresh start. Making changes and starting over can be difficult, though. This spell helps provide the boost needed to take those first steps when starting a new path or journey.

MATERIALS
- Small bowl
- 2 pinches snake track dirt (for new beginnings, rebirth, renewal)
- 2 tablespoons (30 ml) basil (*Ocimum basilicum*) (for breaking blocks, fresh starts, new beginnings)
- 1 tablespoon (15 ml) lemon zest (*Citrus × limon*) (for breaking blocks, new beginnings)
- 2 tablespoons (30 ml) rosemary (*Salvia rosmarinus*) (for new beginnings)
- ½ cup (120 ml) baby powder
- Spoon or wand
- Storage container with a lid
- Pen
- Sticker label

WORKING
1. In the bowl, mix the dirt, herbs, and baby powder together with the spoon or wand. As you stir, repeat the following chant five to seven times:

A fresh start for me, from my past I am free.
By the power of the snake, so shall it be.

2. Once the materials are thoroughly mixed, pour the contents from the bowl to the storage container.

3. Label the container "New Beginnings Powder."

4. Every morning before you head out for the day, sprinkle some of the powder into your shoes. Each step you take during the day will activate the powder and provide the opportunities you need to take the next steps in your life.

Termites

Termites are insects that live in hives underground and in wood, and the wood shavings of a termite nest can be found in a variety of locations, from forests to the middle of a city. With termites, you have the benefit of being able to work with both the dirt from their colonies as well as any of their leavings. The damage done by termites, including the maze of tunnels they leave behind, is why they are primarily associated with baneful magic.

TERMITE SLOW & STEADY DESTRUCTION CURSE

Use this spell when you want to destroy someone or something they have been working on. As with all baneful magic, only consider it after taking all other measures to deal with the individual and the problems at hand. For best results, perform the spell outside, away from your home, and near a trash can.

MATERIALS
- Pen
- Paper
- 3 pinches termite dirt (for decay, destruction)
- 2 crushed snail shells (to cause things to slow down)
- Splash of vinegar (to cause things to go sour)
- 2 pinches poppy seeds (*Papaver somniferum*) (to cause confusion)
- Sharp, pointy stick

WORKING

1. Write out the name of your target on the paper. Include their date of birth if that is known.

2. Underneath your target's name, write out what it is you want destroyed and why. As you write out this information, channel and direct all of your anger and frustrations into the words.

3. Set the paper on the ground, and place the termite dirt on top of the paper. As you add the dirt, state:

   To eat away at work done each day.

4. Sprinkle the snail shells over the dirt. As you do so, state:

   To slow down and pause to see the chaos and all the problems you have caused.

5. Pour the vinegar over the paper. State:

   To make your power taste quite sour.

6. Add the poppy seeds to the paper. State:

   For chaos and confusion.

7. Use the sharp stick to stab the paper several times. With each stab, focus your anger, frustrations, and any other negative emotions you have toward your target into the paper.

8. Once you have thoroughly stabbed the paper, spit on it with malice.

9. Stomp on the paper and grind it into the dirt, tearing it into small pieces.

10. Toss the paper scraps and any other materials into a trash can and walk away. Know that your target will be released once they learn their lesson and approach their life and the situation differently.

TERMITE CONFUSION SPELL

One way to work baneful magic is to cause confusion within an individual's life. This spell uses the energy of termites to do just that.

For safety, perform this spell outside and wear shoes with closed toes.

MATERIALS
- Slip of paper
- Pen

- Small bowl
- Spoon or wand
- 4 pinches termite leavings (for baneful magic)
- ½ tablespoon (7.5 ml) cayenne pepper (*Capsicum annuum*) (for baneful magic)
- 2 tablespoons (30 ml) ground black peppercorn (*Piper nigrum*) (for baneful magic)
- 2 tablespoons (30 ml) galangal root (*Alpinia galanga*) (for justice)
- 1 teaspoon (5 ml) poppy seeds (*Papaver somniferum*) (for chaos, confusion)
- 2 teaspoons (10 ml) mustard seeds (*Brassica juncea*) (for chaos, confusion)
- 2-inch (5-cm) square of white fabric
- 2 pins
- 3 mirror fragments
- 6 inches (15.2 cm) black ribbon or thread

WORKING

1. On the paper, write out the name of your target. If their name is unknown, write out some other way to identify them.

2. In the bowl, mix the termite leavings and herbs together with the wand or spoon. While you stir, state:

   > *For (target's name), chaos, confusion, and pain.*

3. Place the mixture in the center of the white fabric square, and set the slip of paper across the mixture.

4. Stab the pins through the paper. As you stab each one, state:

   I pin you today, that you may not run away.

5. Place the mirror fragments on top of the paper and the herbal mixture. The pieces do not have to face the same way; they just need to be there.

6. Bring the corners of the fabric bundle together and use the black ribbon or thread to tie it shut.

7. Focus all of your anger and frustration into the bundle and smash it on the ground.

8. Carefully pick up the smashed bundle and toss in a trash can far from your home. You can then forget about the spell and return home.

Wolves

Wolves, like snakes, have long been associated with magic and witchcraft. They are cunning, powerful creatures.

WEREWOLF OIL (WOLF SHAPE-SHIFTING OIL)

Shape-shifting has long been associated with witchcraft, witches, and spiritual work. It was believed that witches shape-shifted to travel in secrecy to their rituals and meetings. Wolves are one of the many animals that witches were said to turn into. In some cases, these legends are the origin of werewolf myths. "On their way to the Sabbath the Witches would turn themselves into animals, leaving their bodies behind and traveling 'in the spirit' to the Underworld."[5] Use this oil before engaging in trance work to enhance your experience shape-shifting into a wolf.

This oil takes four to six weeks to create. It will keep for six months.

MATERIALS
- 2 large mason jars with lids
- Mortar and pestle
- Wolf track dirt
- 2 tablespoons (30 ml) basil (*Ocimum basilicum*) (to attract spirits and for spirituality, trance states, underworld work)
- 2 tablespoons (30 ml) damiana leaf (*Turnera diffusa*) (to attract spirits and for spirituality, trance states, underworld work)
- 2 tablespoons (30 ml) wormwood (*Artemisia absinthium*) (to attract spirits and for spirituality, trance states, underworld work)
- ½ tablespoon (7.5 ml) mugwort (*Artemisia vulgaris*) (for meditation, psychic development, spirituality, trance states, underworld work)
- ½ tablespoon (7.5 ml) yarrow (*Achillea millefolium*) (to attract spirits and for spirituality, trance states, underworld work)
- ½ tablespoon (7.5 ml) parsley (*Petroselinum crispum*) (to attract spirits and for meditation, psychic development, spirituality, underworld work)

5. De Vries, *Hedge-Rider*, 98.

- ½ tablespoon (7.5 ml) thyme (*Thymus vulgaris*) (to attract spirits and for meditation, spirituality, trance states, underworld work)
- 16 ounces (500 ml) grape-seed oil
- Cheesecloth
- Pen and label stickers
- Dropper bottle

WORKING

1. Add the wolf track dirt to one of the mason jars.

2. Place the herbal ingredients in the mortar. Use the pestle to grind and mix them together.

3. Once the herbs have been mixed and their oils have been released, scrape the herbs from the mortar and into the jar with the dirt.

4. Fill the jar with the grape-seed oil and seal it.

5. Shake the jar vigorously. As you do so, focus on the essence of the wolf and that spirit being within you. Feel your mind and spirit connect with the mind and spirit of the wolf.

6. Set the jar in a dark and dry place where it can remain undisturbed.

7. Twice daily for the next 4 weeks, shake the jar to stir and activate the herbal mixture. While you shake, recite the following chant five to seven times:

   I call upon the ancient power of the witch.
   Into the shape of a wolf shall my spirit
   shift.

8. After 4 weeks, open the jar. Feel the energy with your hands and spirit. If the energy feels right, then you can begin the next part of the process. If your intuition tells you to wait a few more weeks, seal the jar, put it back where you had it, and continue shaking and chanting twice a day for 2 more weeks.

9. Drape the cheesecloth over the mouth of the second mason jar. Slowly and carefully separate the oil from the herbs by pouring the liquid from the first jar through the cloth and into the second one.

10. Once all of the oil has been poured from the first jar, take the cheesecloth in your hands and squeeze any remaining oil from it.

11. With clean hands, label the second mason jar and the dropper bottle "Wolf Shape-Shifting Oil."

12. Fill the dropper bottle with the charged oil, and dispose of the cheesecloth and herbs in the trash.

13. Before doing any work in the spirit worlds, apply three drops of the oil to your forehead (one at each temple and one in the center) and one drop on each wrist. Know that this oil will help you shift into a wolf's shape while you travel in the spirit worlds.

14. Use your preferred techniques for entering a trance state and engaging in spirit travel. When you enter the trance state, feel your spirit shift

into the shape of a wolf before disappearing into the spirit worlds.

15. After 6 months, dispose of any remaining oil and repeat the process for the next batch.

WOLF FEAR & INTIMIDATION TRAP BOX CHARM

Wolves are intimidating animals. The fact that wolves move in packs gives them strength in numbers, and strength in numbers makes them all the more intimidating. We can use the energy of a wolf pack to intimidate those who would wish us harm. This spell will keep your target trapped until they learn their lesson and repent for what they have done.

For best results, use a wood or ceramic box.

MATERIALS
- Small box that seals
- 5 mirror fragments
- Superglue
- Image of your target or pen and slip of paper
- 1 pinch wolf track dirt
- 1 mandrake root (*Mandragora officinarum*) (to bring fear)
- 1 valerian root (*Valeriana officinalis*) (to cause nightmares)
- ½ teaspoon (2.5 ml) mustard seed (*Brassica juncea*) (for chaos)
- ½ teaspoon (2.5 ml) poppy seed (*Papaver somniferum*) (for confusion)

WORKING

1. Open the box and glue the mirror pieces to its inner sides and bottom. Allow the glue to dry.

2. Once the glue is dry, set the image of your target in the box. If you do not have a photo, write your target's name on the slip of paper and put that in the box.

3. Place the remaining materials in the box one at a time. As you place each item, state why it is being added.

4. Seal and shake the box.

5. Set the box someplace where it will not be disturbed.

6. Twice daily, shake the box to keep the charm activated. Do this until you feel your target has learned their lesson.

7. Once your target has learned their lesson and made an effort to apologize, dispose of the box's contents in the trash. The mirror box can be used for other magical works in the future. Just wash it and coat it with salt to remove the previous energy.

HOME & WORK

Like your clothing or hair, dirt from your home and the places you work contains your personal energy.

Your home is a reflection of yourself, as well as anyone else who lives there, and it is where you are most protected, have the most power, and can let your guard down. Magically, the dirt from your home can be used to influence and protect the people who live there. As well as holding the energy of everyone within the home, the dirt also contains the essence of the home's spirit.

Similarly, spirits also reside where people work. Each of these spirits is a combination of energy taken from the individuals who work there and the energy of what happens there. Any dirt gathered from a workspace can be used to impact that business, the customers, and its employees.

Spirit of the Home

All homes have at least one spirit that resides within them. A single-family house has one spirit. Multifamily dwellings will have multiple spirits, each apartment or unit developing its own unique spirit. Everyone within a single home, whether that home is an apartment unit or a house, works with the same spirit.

The spirit of your home has its own personality—its own likes, wants, and desires—and it is important to get to know the spirit of your home. When you have a relationship with the spirit, things go much smoother.

The spirit of your home is not the same as the spirit of the land that your home is on. These two spirits often work together and are often honored as one, but the spirit of your home and the spirit of its land are separate beings. The spirit of the land is the combined essence of all plants and animals within the land, while the spirit of the hearth and home is made up of a combination of the land spirit and the essence of those living in the home.

There are many ways you can get to know the spirit of your home. The easiest way is to simply talk to them. Tell the spirit about your day. Say good morning and good evening to your home. These small actions go a long way in getting to know the spirit of your home.

As you converse with your home, you may find out that the spirit of the house has a name. If you do, use it.

Reclaiming that name will almost immediately make a difference in the atmosphere and feeling of the home. If your home doesn't have a name, you can give it one. The gift of a name is an offering that also works as a bonding tool between you and the spirit.

This may seem silly, but it is effective. Spiritual and magical work does occasionally look and feel silly, and that is okay. You can have fun and be silly while still having respect and a sincere approach to a topic. This can help you to relax a bit and become more comfortable with the work of magic. Storm Faerywolf put it accurately in his book *The Witch's Name* when he said:

> *It's okay if it makes you feel silly, at first. Magic is ludicrous. When we get comfortable with the idea of silliness then we can move beyond it and into the area of the powers which we have been seeking; we can start the process of weaving these elements together and create something that is magically greater than just the sum of its component parts.*[6]

GET TO KNOW YOUR HOME

This exercise goes a long way when it comes to getting to know the spirit and essence of your home. The best rooms for this exercise are the kitchen and living room. For best results, this meditation

6. Faerywolf, *The Witch's Name*, 80.

should be recorded before hand and then played back. If recording is not an option, then the meditation should be read out loud by another willing individual.

Make sure your windows are open for ventilation. The recipe for spirit offering incense can be found in part 3.

MATERIALS
- Notebook
- Pen
- White taper candle
- Candleholder
- Censer and heat pad
- Self-lighting charcoal disc
- Tongs
- Long-stemmed lighter
- 1 tablespoon (15 ml) spirit offering incense
- Soft music, optional

WORKING
1. Clean the area you are going to do this working in thoroughly. Make sure any clutter is minimal. Also make sure you will be undisturbed during the work. If anyone enters the room, they must be quiet and respectful.

2. Find a safe spot to set the candle and the censer. Put the candle in its holder. Place the censer and heat pad next to it. If you are going to have music playing, now is the time to start it.

3. Use the tongs to hold the charcoal, and use the long-stemmed lighter to light it. Once the charcoal is glowing softly around the edges and sparks have gone across the disc, it is ready to be used. Carefully place the charcoal in the censer.

4. Get seated. Make sure you are comfortable and in a relaxed state. Take a few deep breaths to ground and center.

5. Light the candle and sprinkle the incense over the charcoal. As you do so, state:

   Spirit of my home, I call on you today. Help me to know you. Let me hear what you have to say.

6. Take a few deep breaths. Inhale for the count of four. Hold your breath for a count of four, and exhale for a count of four. Continue to use this breathing pattern until you reach a light meditative state.

   When you enter the light meditative state, sense or feel in your mind's eye a portal to the spirit realm in front of you. Walk through the portal.

   As you exit the portal, see, sense, or feel yourself standing in front of your home. Standing in front of you is the spirit of your home.

   When you see the spirit of your home, introduce yourself to them. Ask them for their name and for them to tell you about them.

Listen to what the spirit has to say. Try to remember everything that you learn from them. When you have had a small conversation with the spirit, thank the spirit for their time and walk back through the portal. Slowly come back to your normal waking consciousness.

7. In your notebook, write down everything that you experienced.

8. Going forward, whenever you want to talk to the spirit of your home, just speak out loud. You have met them, and they have met you in the spirit world.

CREATION OF A HEARTH & HOME ALTAR

Another way you can get to know the spirit of your home is through creating a small altar or shrine for it. An altar shows that you respect the spirit as an individual and not just as an object you live in.

An altar also gives the spirit a physical place to reside and stay, allowing them to simply rest. It will feel like home to them and make them happy. Creating an altar is a gift to the spirit. It will also provide a place for you to leave offerings to them.

These altars don't need to be very complicated. For the spirit of the hearth and home, a simple altar is the way to go. They are easy to care for and can be hidden in plain sight.

MATERIALS

- Small coffee table, shelf, or other flat surface to work as the altar
- Miniature hand broom
- Cleaning supplies
- Washcloth
- White or decorative cloth
- White pillar candle
- Candleholder
- Censer and heat pad
- Small plate
- Decorative shot glass
- Framed photos of household members, including pets and anyone staying in the home for a period of time
- Self-lighting charcoal disc
- 1 tablespoon (15 ml) spirit offering incense
- Long-stemmed lighter
- Lighter or matches

WORKING

1. Use the miniature broom to spiritually cleanse and clear the chosen altar space of all other energetic forces. See, feel, or otherwise sense the energy being brushed off and away.

2. Once the space has been spiritually cleansed, use the cleaning supplies to cleanse it physically. Let the space dry if necessary.

3. Use the white or decorative cloth to cover the altar and make it look nice.

4. Set the candle in its holder and place it on the center of the altar. Place the censer and heat pad next to the candle. Behind the candle and censer, place the small plate. Set the shot glass beside the plate.

5. Around the other materials, place the framed photos. Arrange them in ways that look appealing to you, using them to hide the altar tools if necessary. Your altar is now ready to be used.

6. Take the charcoal disc with the tongs. Use the long-stemmed lighter to light the charcoal. Once the charcoal is glowing around all of the corners, carefully return the disc to the censer. Sprinkle a little of the incense over the charcoal disc. Light the candle. State:

   Spirit of the hearth and home, I created this shrine for you today. May it be a place for you to rest and renew.

7. If you know the name of the spirit of your home, use it to call on them now. If the house does not have a name, this is the time to give it one.

8. Let the incense and candle burn for a little while (15 to 30 minutes). While they burn, focus on your connection with the spirit of your home, then extinguish the candle and incense.

9. Tend to the altar at least once a week. See the following exercise for some ideas how.

RITUAL TO TEND TO THE HEARTH & HOME ALTAR

Now that the altar has been created, it's time to start tending to it and feeding the spirit of the home. Each offering you give the spirit feeds it energy, nourishing the spirit. The best offering is a bit of liquor, like vodka or rum, and a piece of bread or a biscuit. Both of these are considered traditional offerings to spirits. You can also offer charms that you make, your favorite foods—anything really.

As long as the spirit is fed and remembered, they will treat you well, help you, and protect you and your family. Use these steps to tend to the altar you created with the previous exercise. For best results, tend to the altar once a week.

MATERIALS
- Cleaning supplies
- Self-lighting charcoal disc
- Tongs
- Long-stemmed lighter
- 1 tablespoon (15 ml) spirit offering incense
- Offering/gift

WORKING
1. Remove any old offerings on the altar. If possible, biodegradable offerings should be buried and returned to the earth. When that is not possible, offerings may be disposed of in the trash. If the

candle has burned out, replace it with a fresh one and put the old candle in the trash.

2. Clean any dust or dirt from the altar. If there are items that don't belong there, remove them.

3. Hold the charcoal disc with the tongs, and use the long-stemmed lighter to light the charcoal. Once the charcoal is glowing softly and sparks have spread across the disc, carefully place it in the censer.

4. Light the candle and sprinkle the incense over the charcoal.

5. Speak to the spirit of your home. Let them know of any issues currently in your life and what is going well.

6. After the conversation has ended, place any liquid offerings in the shot glass. All other offerings should be placed on the plate.

7. Extinguish the candle and incense and return to your day-to-day life.

Working with Dirt from Your Home

You have created an altar and established a relationship with the spirit of your home. Now that these basics have been covered, it's time to start talking about the magic we can do with a little dirt from the home. Remember that as well as representing your home as an energetic force and living spirit, any dirt harvested from your home can be used as a personal effect to impact you or those who live with you.

PROTECT YOUR HOME WHILE AWAY PACKET SPELL

This spell is ideal for when you will be traveling and away from your home for a week or more. It will provide protection while you are gone.

MATERIALS
- Paper
- Pen
- 2 teaspoons (10 ml) of dirt from your home (connection to your home)
- 1 teaspoon (5 ml) ground black peppercorn (*Piper nigrum*) (for protection)
- 1 foot (30.5 cm) black ribbon

WORKING
1. On the paper, draw a basic floor plan of your home. In the middle of the floor plan, write down your wish for your home to be protected while you are away.

2. Sprinkle the dirt and the black peppercorn across the floor plan. As you do so, recite the following chant three to five times:

    Protect this home while away I roam.

3. Fold the paper in half toward you. Repeat this fold four times. Each time you fold the paper, recite the previous chant.

4. Wrap the ribbon around the paper several times, saying the previous chant each time. After wrapping the paper at least three times, tie a knot to seal the packet.

5. Carry the packet with you in your purse, pocket, or bag while traveling. This will keep your home protected.

6. When you return home, scatter the dirt and black peppercorn around the outside of your home and toss the paper in the trash.

PEACEFUL HOME POWDER

This spell helps bring peace to your home, and it can also be used for other people and their homes. As always, make sure you have consent before casting a spell for another person.

MATERIALS
- Mortar and pestle
- ¼ teaspoon (1.5 ml) dirt from the home that needs peace (connection to that home)
- 1 teaspoon (5 ml) lavender (*Lavandula angustifolia*) (for family, home, peace)
- 1 teaspoon (5 ml) chamomile (*Matricaria recutita*) (for happiness, peace)
- 1 teaspoon (5 ml) rosemary (*Salvia rosmarinus*) (for family, peaceful home)
- Small container with lid
- Pen and label sticker

WORKING

1. Use the mortar and pestle to mix the dirt and herbs. Grind the herbs into as fine of a powder as you possibly can. While you grind and mix, recite the following chant five to seven times or until you have a well-ground blend of herbs and dirt:

   Peace and serenity within the home.

2. Move the mixture into the container. Label it "Peaceful Home Dirt." If you are working the spell for someone else, the label should read "(Name)'s Peaceful Home Dirt."

3. Go outside and sprinkle the mixture around the foundation of your home. For those living in multifamily houses, sprinkle the dirt along the walls of your unit, starting with the living room. As you sprinkle the dirt, repeat the peace and serenity chant. When performing this spell for another person, keep the mixture in storage until you visit their home. On your next visit, before entering the residence, sprinkle the mixture as you would for your own home.

4. Repeat step 3 once a month for continued peace.

PROSPEROUS HOME PACKET SPELL

Use this spell to bring prosperity and financial security to your home.

MATERIALS

- Quarter
- Dollar bill
- Pinch of dirt from your home (for connection to the home)
- 1 teaspoon (5 ml) sugar (for attraction)

WORKING

1. Place the quarter in the center of the dollar bill.

2. Sprinkle the dirt over the quarter.

3. Cover the dirt and quarter with the sugar. As you do so, state:

    Sugar, sweetly attract money freely.

4. Fold the dollar bill around the coin, creating a small packet with the quarter, dirt, and sugar at the center.

5. Carry this packet in your pocket or in your wallet with your cash. As long as you carry it, you should have financial success and security.

Working with Dirt from Another Home

When you do not have access to personal effects for an individual, you can use dirt from their home just as you would the dirt from their foot tracks. Remember the laws regarding trespassing. You need to have permission from the person who owns the land to be there. Also remember that—with the exception of baneful workings—whenever you do magic for another person, you must get their consent. Without their consent, you are imposing your will on them, and that is unethical.

HEAL A FRIEND PAPER POPPET SPELL

This is a spell for general health and wellness blessings. It does not target, heal, or treat any specific ailment. For their best health, your loved one must go through with regular checkups with their doctor and other medical professionals.

MATERIALS
- 2 pieces of paper
- Pen
- Scissors
- Pin, needle, or knife
- Blue candle
- Lighter or matches
- Candleholder
- Dirt from your friend's home (for connection to your friend and as a personal effect of your friend)
- 1 teaspoon (5 ml) lavender (*Lavandula angustifolia*) (for healing)
- 1 teaspoon (5 ml) marigold (*Calendula officinalis*) (for healing)
- 1 teaspoon (5 ml) mint (*Mentha*) (for healing)

WORKING
1. Put the two pieces of paper on top of each other. On the paper, draw a human shape. Using scissors, cut out the shape, cutting through both

pieces of paper. On one of the figures, write your friend's name and date of birth. On the other figure, write the words "Health and Wellness Boost."

2. Use the pin, needle, or knife to carve your friend's name into the candle.

3. Light the candle and carefully use the melting wax to seal the two human shapes together with the words facing out. Seal all edges but the head. When the poppet is mostly sealed, place the candle in the holder.

4. Add the dirt and herbs to the poppet in any order, and finish sealing the poppet with wax.

5. Shake the poppet to mix the herbs and dirt. As you shake, recite the following chant three times:

   Health and wellness today. A healing boost sent (friend's name)'s way.

6. Place the poppet safely in front of the candle-holder. Recite the following chant three to five times:

   Candle of blue, burning bright, by your light healing flows to (friend's name) this night.

7. Burn the candle for 10 minutes, visualizing a healing light surrounding your friend. After 10 minutes, extinguish the candle and place the poppet under the candleholder.

8. Every day for the next week, spend 10 minutes lighting the candle, reciting the candle chant three to five times. If your candle finishes burning before the end of the week, use another blue candle, carving your friend's name into it as well.

9. At the end of the week, dispose of the candle and poppet in the trash. Know that your friend now has a healing boost sent their way and will experience a run of better health.

ATTRACT NEW OPPORTUNITIES CHARM

Sometimes we need a little help finding the courage to try new things. By working this spell, you will help a friend open up to new opportunities and increase the chances they will have new experiences.

MATERIALS
- Skeleton key (to open doors)
- Small container with lid
- Small bowl
- Spoon or wand
- ¼ cup (60 ml) dirt from your friend's home (as a personal effect of your friend)
- 1 tablespoon (15 ml) basil (*Ocimum basilicum*) (for block busting, road opening)
- 1 tablespoon (15 ml) rosemary (*Salvia rosmarinus*) (for block busting, cleansing)
- 1 tablespoon (15 ml) sugar (for attraction)

- Key ring
- Necklace chain

WORKING

1. Place the key in the bottom of the container.

2. In the bowl, use the spoon or wand to mix the dirt, herbs, and sugar together. While you stir, recite the following chant five times:

   Saint Peter, opener of the gateway, open new roads for (your friend's name) today.

3. Cover the key with the dirt, herb, and sugar mixture.

4. Close the container.

5. Hold the container tightly. While you do so, shake the container to charge and mix the materials. As you shake, recite St. Peter's prayer five times:

   O God, who hast given unto Thy blessed Apostle Peter the keys to thy kingdom of heaven, and the power to bind and loose: grant that we may be delivered, through the help of his intercession, from the slavery to all our sins: Who livest and reignest world without end.[7]

6. Once a day for the next week, shake the container gently, knowing that your friend will have new opportunities come their way. While

---

7. "St. Peter," Catholic Online.

shaking the container, recite St. Peter's prayer
five times.

7. After a week, take the key from the container.
   Put it on a key ring and thread that key ring onto
   the necklace chain.

8. Give the charm to your friend and tell them to
   hang it by the front door. Every time the door
   is opened, the charm will be activated and the
   energy sent out into the universe.

ENHANCE LOVE CANDLE SPELL

This spell will bring love into your friend's life.
They may find new love, or they may reconnect
with old friends. The goal is simply to make them
feel and know that they are loved.

MATERIALS
- Medium red taper candle
- Pin, needle, or knife
- Small bowl
- Spoon or wand
- Dirt from your friend's home (as a personal effect
  of your friend)
- 1 tablespoon (15 ml) red rose petals (*Rosa*)
  (for love)
- 1 tablespoon (15 ml) patchouli leaf (*Pogostemon
  cablin*) (for love, sexuality)
- 1 tablespoon (15 ml) juniper (*Juniperus communis*)
  (for love, protection of love)
- 1 tablespoon (15 ml) olive oil

- Small plate
- Candleholder
- Lighter or matches

WORKING

1. Use the pin, needle, or knife to carve your friend's name into one side of the candle. On the other side, write the words "Enhance Love."

2. In the bowl, use the spoon or wand to mix the dirt and the herbs together. As you stir, recite the following chant five times:

    Love for (target's name). Love that's new, love that's true.

3. Anoint the candle with the oil from bottom to top to attract and grow love.

4. Pour the dirt and herb mixture onto the plate. Roll the candle in the mixture, coating the candle in it.

5. Put the candleholder on the plate and place the candle in the holder.

6. Light the candle. As the candle burns, recite the following chant five to seven times:

    Red candle, burning bright, with your sacred light bring love to (friend's name) tonight. A love that is true and right.

7. Let the candle burn out. If you are unable to burn the candle completely in one sitting, burn the candle for 5 minutes once a day, reciting the

chant five times, until the candle has burned completely.

8. Once the candle has burned down, dispose of the candle and herbal mixture in a trash can near your friend's home.

Using Dirt from Your Place of Work

You can also use dirt from where you work (or would like to work) to perform spells that impact your time there or the business itself. In these cases, dirt, again, works like a personal effect. This time, the dirt can be a substitute for business cards or job applications. You do not need consent to do this type of work. You still need to be mindful of trespassing laws, though. You must also still give an offering to the spirit of the building before taking the dirt.

ATTRACT COWORKERS SPELL

Sometimes the search for new coworkers can take too long. This spell helps speed up the process and attract people who actually want the job, not those just seeking any job. This spell can easily be adapted by substituting the word "coworker" for "employee."

MATERIALS
- Small bowl
- 1½ tablespoons (22.5 ml) of dirt from where you work (as a connection to your place of work)

- ¼ tablespoon (4 ml) sugar (for attraction)
- ¼ tablespoon (4 ml) rosemary (*Salvia rosmarinus*) (to open the mind)
- ¼ tablespoon (4 ml) masterwort (*Astrantia major*) (for control, persuasion)
- ¼ tablespoon (4 ml) yellow marigold petals (*Calendula officinalis*) (for employment, money)
- ¼ tablespoon (4 ml) cayenne pepper (*Capsicum annuum*) (for speed)
- ¼ tablespoon (4 ml) cinnamon (*Cinnamomum verum*) (for attraction, employment, money)
- Spoon or wand
- Small plastic baggie

WORKING

1. Begin adding the dirt and herbal materials, including the sugar, to the bowl, starting with ¼ tablespoon of dirt. Then add one of the herbal materials. Between each herbal material, add ¼ more tablespoon of dirt. As you add each ingredient, state why you are using it.

2. Use the spoon or wand to mix the materials together. While you stir, visualize and focus on having a workplace full of positive coworkers who want to be there. See yourself and your workplace being prosperous and successful thanks to the filled positions. Direct that energy into the mixture and recite the following chant five times for each material:

   Coworkers new, faithful, and true, working willingly, bringing peace and prosperity.

3. Pour the mixture into the baggie. The next time you go to work, take the mix with and sprinkle some of it across the doorway and walkway. As you sprinkle the material, state:

   For those who true employment seek, may here you find what you seek.

4. Toss the baggie in the trash and go about your workday.

PREVENT NEGATIVE CUSTOMER REVIEW SPELL

This spell is a variation of a spell I mentioned in the introduction, which I performed after I realized the customer service I provided could have negative results. Use this spell to protect your work place from negative reviews or problematic comments based on work you performed.

MATERIALS
- Spoon or wand
- Small bowl
- 2 teaspoons (10 ml) dirt from where you work (as a connection to your place of work)
- 1 teaspoon (5 ml) ground black peppercorn (*Piper nigrum*) (for protection)
- 1 teaspoon (5 ml) ground galangal root (*Alpinia galanga*) (for protection, reversal)
- 1 teaspoon (5 ml) ground angelica root (*Angelica archangelica*) (for protection)
- Small baggie

WORKING

1. Use the spoon or wand to mix the dirt and herbs in the bowl. As you stir, chant seven to nine times:

   Protect (where you work) from a bad review. Let them see the best service known to be true.

2. Pour the mixture into the baggie.

3. Take the bag to work and sprinkle half of the mixture across the entrance. Sprinkle the other half at a stop sign nearby. As you scatter the mixture, visualize a shield covering the place you work, stopping any potential bad reviews from being shared or posted publicly.

LISTEN TO ME SPELL

Use this spell when you need to talk to your boss about something. The working will encourage them to listen, open their mind to your view, and increase the likelihood that you will get what you need.

MATERIALS
- Paper
- Pen
- Small plate
- Pin, needle, or knife
- Blue votive candle
- Olive oil
- Small bowl

- Spoon or wand
- 2 teaspoons (15 ml) dirt from your work (as a connection to your place of work)
- 2 tablespoons (30 ml) rosemary (*Salvia rosmarinus*) (to open the mind)
- 1 tablespoon (15 ml) sugar (for sweetening)
- 1 tablespoon (15 ml) masterwort (*Astrantia major*) (for persuasion)
- 1 tablespoon (15 ml) ginkgo leaf (*Ginkgo biloba*) (to focus, open the mind)
- Lighter or matches

WORKING

1. On the paper, write out what you are trying to get your boss to hear. Include all of the important details. If it helps, you can even write a "script" of sorts.

2. Put the plate on top of the paper. Use the pin, needle, or knife to carve the words "Listen to Me" into the candle. Place the candle on the plate, using the plate as a candleholder.

3. Anoint the candle from the bottom to the top with the olive oil, stating:

   Listen to me.

4. In the bowl, use the spoon or wand to mix the dirt, herbs, and sugar together. As you mix, recite the following chant seven to nine times:

   Herbs open the way so that (your boss's name) will hear what I have to say.

5. Sprinkle the mixture around the base of the candle, reciting the same chant from step 4 three to five times or until you run out of the mixture.

6. Light the candle and state:

   Candle burning bright, your flames light the way this night.

7. As the candle burns, visualize yourself having the desired conversation with your boss. See them understanding what you have to say and doing what they can to accommodate you. Hold those images for as long as you can and direct that energy into the candle.

8. Let the candle burn until finished. If you cannot burn the candle in a single sitting, burn the candle for 5 to 10 minutes every day until the candle has burned out completely.

9. Once the candle has burned out, dispose of everything but the plate in a trash can near your work.

NATURAL LOCATIONS

The world we live in has a variety of lands and environments, and each location has its own unique magical energy. Natural locations are easier to pull power from than urban locations. This is because their energy is purer. Urban locations are highly flavored by the actions—and inactions—that occur there, while locations in nature are largely left alone to do what they will.

When harvesting dirt from natural locations, remember to adhere to laws regarding land use. Make sure you do not gather dirt from protected landmasses.

You must also remember that respect for the land, its spirit, and the creatures living there is essential. Always make sure your offerings are suitable for nature. Find out what foods are toxic to local wildlife.

This chapter is not meant to be a comprehensive guide to natural locations but a starting point. I will cover some of the most common natural locations, and the magical associations that I list come from both folklore and personal experience. If the associations do not work for you, try your own correspondences instead. As always, take notes.

Mountains

Let's begin with mountain energy. Mountains are tall and powerful and overlook large areas. Mountain ranges provide homes for a variety of wildlife, including bears, mountain lions, lynx, deer, hawks, and squirrels. When you consider the animals that live on mountains and the protection mountains provide, it is easy to see how safety and strength are two of its magical properties.

Mountaintops have clean and clear air, and on cloudless days, you can see for an extended range. When it comes to magic and spirituality, clear sight can be translated into psychic sight and spiritual powers. Use some dirt from a mountain top to strengthen your gifts and abilities.

When gathering mountaintop dirt, only climb as high as you safely can. Dirt gathered at that height will be good enough.

Mountain Protection Charm

Use this spell to create a portable protection charm that calls upon the powers of the mountain to protect you throughout daily life.

If you don't have hematite, you can use any other black stone chips instead.

MATERIALS
- Small glass vial
- 1 teaspoon (5 ml) sea salt (to absorb negativity and neutralize unwanted energy)
- 1 teaspoon (5 ml) hematite chips (to protect against unwanted energy and reflect and return unwanted energy)
- 2 pinches dirt from the foot of a mountain (for protection)
- 2 pinches dirt from the top of the same mountain (for protection)
- Hot glue gun and glue

WORKING
1. In the small vial, place the tumbles or chips, the salt, and the mountain dirt. Seal the vial with hot glue.

2. Once the glue has dried, shake the vial to mix the materials. As you shake, feel the dirt absorb the energies of the crystals and salt, using them to enhance its own protective energy. Feel the energy pulsate into your hands and around your

body, enveloping you in a shield that looks like a mountain.

3. Once you have finished shaking the vial, place it in your pocket or find a way to carry the charm with you. The charm will provide protection as long as the vial is sealed.

4. When you no longer feel the need for extra protection, unseal the vial. Dispose of the dirt and salt in the trash. Set the stone chips aside. Next time you go to the mountain, place the chips somewhere as an offering to the mountain spirit.

MOUNTAINSIDE CLEAR SIGHT ENCHANTMENT

Use this spell to charge your favorite tarot deck or divination tool with mountain dirt.

The pouch used should be big enough to fit your chosen tool.

MATERIALS
- Small bowl
- Spoon or wand
- 2 pinches mountaintop dirt (for clear sight)
- 1 tablespoon (15 ml) mugwort (*Artemisia vulgaris*) (for psychic development)
- 1 tablespoon (15 ml) eyebright (*Euphrasia rostkoviana*) (for divination)
- 1 tablespoon (15 ml) wormwood (*Artemisia absinthium*) (for divination, psychic development)

- Silver or purple pouch
- Chosen divination tool

WORKING

1. In the bowl, use the spoon or wand to mix the mountain dirt with the herbs, reciting the following chant five to seven times:

   Dirt from the mountaintop high, grant me psychic sight through my third eye.

2. As you mix and chant, feel the energy for psychic sight and psychic development flowing from the materials and creating a cohesive force. Visualize a purple light glowing from and surrounding the mixture.

3. Once you feel that the mixture is as charged as possible, pour half into the small pouch.

4. Rub the other half of the mixture on your divination tool. As you do so, feel the power of clear sight pass into it, enhancing the tool's connection to your intuition and psychic sight.

5. Return the tool to the pouch. Hold the pouch up to the center of your forehead, where your psychic eye sits. As you hold the pouch there, feel the energy of the tool and powder pulsating together as one. Sense your psychic eye opening and getting stronger. Know that the power flowing from the pouch will enhance and strengthen your psychic senses and connection with this tool.

6. Place the pouch in your pillowcase, beneath your pillow, to enhance your psychic dreams and connection to psychic sight.

TO CREATE AN IMMOVABLE FORCE CURSE

Mountains are immovable. To get through mountains, people must use explosives, and traveling over them takes time and effort. Transfer this powerful energy to spellwork for your benefit.

If someone has been harassing you, you can use this spell to prevent them from getting anything done at all. It will essentially put their life to a stop until you decide they have learned their lesson.

MATERIALS
- Paper
- Pen
- Small plastic container
- Handful of mountain dirt (to create blocks)
- Handful of rocks and stones from the mountain path (to create blocks)

WORKING
1. On the paper, write out your target's name and date of birth. If their name or date of birth is not known, write out any identifying information you can. The better you can identify your target, the better the spell will work.

2. Tear the paper into shreds and place them in the container.

3. Sprinkle the mountain dirt over the paper shreds. As you sprinkle the dirt, state:

   Mountain dirt, strong and true, to my target create obstacles that are new.

4. Place the rocks on top of your target's name, forcing them to stay in place.

5. Every day, move the stones around the container, keeping the name covered by at least one rock at all times.

6. When you are ready to release your target, move any rocks from on top of the paper shreds and burn the paper. Scatter the remaining dirt and rocks at various crossroads, releasing the energy.

Volcanoes

Another ancient primal force is that of the volcano. Volcanos have very explosive energy. That explosive energy can be used for beneficial work as well as baneful and destructive work.

Anger and stress can be explosive emotions that are often associated with volcanic forces. Volcanic explosions work as a pressure valve for the inner stress of our planet. Tap into that imagery and energy to help relieve your own stress and frustrations.

In addition to the dirt around volcanoes, the ash from a volcano can also be worked with effectively.

When gathering this powerful dirt, do so when the volcanoes are dormant. Never approach lava. If it is not practical to gather volcanic dirt or ash, you can order it online.

RELEASE FRUSTRATIONS CLEANSING SPELL

Sometimes when we are stressed and frustrated, it can be difficult to see the solutions to the problems at hand. The following spell calls on the power of volcanoes to help us relieve some stress in a safe and beneficial way.

This spell involves burning paper. For safety, perform this working in an outdoor area cleared of debris. Have a fire extinguisher or bowl of water nearby.

MATERIALS
- Paper
- Pen
- Firesafe bowl
- Lighter or matches
- Spoon or wand
- Pinch of volcano dirt (for stress relief)
- Fire extinguisher or bowl of water

WORKING
1. Clear your outdoor work area of any debris. Set the fire extinguisher or bowl of water within hand's reach.

2. On the paper, write out all of the things that are causing you stress, anxiety, and frustration right now.

3. Tear the paper into tiny pieces, directing your anger, stress, and frustration into it.

4. Throw the pieces of paper in the bowl, and light them on fire. As the paper burns, feel your stress, frustration, and anxiety being relieved.

5. Once the paper has burned to ash and cooled, mix in the volcano dirt. As you stir in the dirt, state:

   Pressure valve of the earth today, release the pressure inside me I pray. My stress and anxiety shall not stay.

6. Bring the mixture to a stop sign and sprinkle the mix around it, stating:

   With this power, stress is stopped this hour.

7. Return home and go about your day, forgetting about your stressors and problems. The next day you should feel a lot less stressed and begin to find solutions to your problems.

RETURN TO SENDER PROTECTION SPELL

Volcanic ash and obsidian are powerful tools when it comes to defensive work. They can be used in banishment and removal spells as well as in curses, hexes, and reversal work.

Use this spell to protect your home from magical attacks and return them to their sender.

MATERIALS
- Small bowl
- Spoon or wand
- 2 pinches volcanic ash or 2 small obsidian tumbles (for protection)
- 2 tablespoons (30 ml) sea salt (to absorb attacks)
- 2 tablespoons (30 ml) ground black peppercorn (*Piper nigrum*) (to return to sender)
- 1 tablespoon (15 ml) cayenne pepper (*Capsicum annuum*) (to return to sender)
- Small storage container with lid
- Pen and label sticker
- Broom

WORKING
1. In the bowl, mix the ash or tumbles, salt, and herbs. As you stir, recite the following statement three times:

   Volcanic earth today, return any negativity sent our way. Protect us from magical attack and send it back.

2. Transfer the dirt mixture to the storage container. Seal the container and label it "Return to Sender Powder."

3. Sprinkle the powder across your home's entrances and windows. As you sprinkle the mixture, feel a reflective barrier encompass your

home. This barrier will repel magical attacks and ill wishes. This shield will last one week.

4. After one week, use the broom to sweep up the mixture, removing the old barrier, and sprinkle a new barrier. Repeat this cycle of sweeping and sprinkling until the attack has passed or you no longer feel ill will being directed toward you and your family. Any remaining powder can be saved and used as needed in the future.

BLAST THROUGH BLOCKS
ROAD-OPENING WORKING

Use this spell to blast through and overcome any obstacles that stand in your way.

You can substitute the volcanic dirt with basalt, volcanic ash, or several lava stones.

MATERIALS
- Pen
- Paper
- Scissors
- 2 bay leaves (*Laurus nobilis*) (for block busting, door opening)
- 2 teaspoons (10 ml) volcano dirt (to overcome obstacles)

WORKING
1. On the paper, write a list of the blocks and obstacles that are keeping you from accomplishing your goal. Leave a space between each block.

2. Cut the paper into strips, leaving each block on its own strip.

3. Write the words "Block Buster" on one bay leaf and "Road Opener" on the other.

4. Place the bay leaves on top of the slips of paper.

5. Sprinkle the volcano dirt over the slips of paper. As you sprinkle the dirt, state:

   By the power of the volcano's explosive nature, all blocks in my path are blown away.

6. Visualize all of the obstacles being blown away and a clear path forward appearing before you.

7. Leave the pile as is for 1 to 2 weeks. After 1 to 2 weeks, dispose of all the materials in a trash can, knowing that you will overcome all your obstacles.

Forests & Woods

One of my favorite pastimes as a child was playing in forested areas, and I would spend all day exploring the woods behind my home. The privacy made me feel like I was living in a forest hut from fairy tales. Today, seeing trees brings me comfort, and I feel safe and protected when I am surrounded by them. I always feel better when there are trees surrounding my home. One way to keep the protective and comforting energy of the forest and woods is to use dirt taken from them in your spellwork.

Home Protection Charm

Use this spell to create a protective ward for your home. This spell works for all homes—no matter what or where they are.

MATERIALS
- Small bowl
- Spoon or wand
- 3 tablespoons (45 ml) dirt from the forest (for protection)
- 3 tablespoons (45 ml) dirt from your home (as a connection to your home)
- 2 tablespoons (30 ml) sea salt (for neutralization of unwanted energy, protection)

WORKING
1. In the bowl, use the spoon or wand to mix both types of dirt with the salt. As you stir, recite any protection prayers or chants you favor three times. You can say something along the lines of:

   Protection for my home on this day. That which is unwanted cannot stay.

2. Take the bowl outside, and starting at your front door, walk clockwise around the outside of your home, sprinkling the mixture. As you scatter the mixture, visualize your home being surrounded by a protective wall of trees. Only you and those you choose to let in can get through.

3. When you return to your front door, draw a pentacle over the doorway with your dominant hand and state:

> **By the power of the woods and trees, the house will protected be. No harm shall be able to reach me.**

4. Once a month, sprinkle more of the dirt mixture around your home to maintain the protective ward.

HEDGE-WALKING TRANCE CHARM

Magicians and witches have long been known to be able to walk between multiple realms, the mundane world of our day-to-day lives and the realms of the gods, the realms of spirits, and the realms of the dead. Hedge witchcraft is a style of witchcraft that focuses on using those skills. All witches have the power to travel in the spiritual worlds. Using the energy from wooded areas is one way to do so.

One of the reasons forests are considered transitional spaces, with access to both the heavens and the underworld, is the fact that trees span the three worlds. Trees reach to the heavens (realms of the gods and spirits) with their branches. Tree trunks exist here in the mundane world. The roots extend into the underworld. By traveling up or down the trunk of a tree in the forest, we can travel to these worlds freely. Use this charm to help you perform trance work on the go. This work involves a short guided meditation. For best results, record the meditation and play it back when you do the actual work. If recording the meditation is not an option, have someone read it aloud to you.

MATERIALS
- Small glass vial with miniature cork stopper
- 2 pinches forest dirt (for spirit world energy, trance work)
- Pinch of wormwood (*Artemisia absinthium*) (for trance work)
- Pinch of damiana leaf (*Turnera diffusa*) (for psychic development, spirit work)
- Pinch of mugwort (*Artemisia vulgaris*) (for psychic development, spirit work)
- Notebook

WORKING
1. Add the dirt and herbs to the vial.

2. Place the cork stopper in the vial and shake the vial to mix the herbs and dirt together. As you shake, recite the following chant seven to nine times:

   Forests, land of spirits, hear my plea. Let me walk in your land freely.

3. Hold the charm in your hand and take four deep breaths. Use these four breaths to ground and focus on the work at hand. When you are ready, listen to the following meditation.

   Close your eyes and relax. Take a deep breath and slowly exhale. Slowly begin to count back from thirteen to one, visualizing the numbers as you count down. When you reach one, you are at a gentle and light meditative state.

Begin to count back from twelve to one, this time without seeing the numbers. Relax and feel yourself enter a deeper meditative state. When you reach one focus on the vial in your hand.

See and feel a large forest filled with lush trees spring up from the vial in front of you. Reach out to one of the trees and feel your energy merge with the tree. You can now freely travel to the heavens with the gods or into the underworld and visit with the ancestors. Take your time and travel to either the heavens or the underworld.

When you have finished your spirit work, see yourself emerge from the tree. Bow before the tree as a thank you for this time.

Begin to count up from one to twelve. When you reach twelve, watch the forest return to the vial as if it had never been there. Slowly count up from one to thirteen. When you reach thirteen, wiggle your fingers and toes to bring awareness back to your body. Once you open your eyes, you have fully returned to your body.

4. Direct any remaining mental and spiritual energy from the meditation into the vial. This will charge the vial with psychic energy, allowing you to use it as a tool to travel the spiritual realms.

5. Ground and center by placing your fingers on the ground and push out any energy or sensations remaining from your meditation experience.

6. Once you have fully become aware of your surroundings, record your experiences in a journal.

7. Store the charm with your other ritual supplies. To recharge it, shake the charm and recite the chant from step 2 seven to nine times. Anytime you want to travel through the spiritual worlds, you simply need to hold on to the vial and focus on the energy within.

To Cause Nightmares Hex

Forests can be a place of fear, and in medieval times, the forest was home to the unseen and unknown. This fear can be used to teach those who have abused, harassed, or caused you harm a lesson.

Use this spell to cause someone who has wronged your family to have terrible nightmares until they learn their lesson. For safety, this spell must be performed outside in an area cleared of any flammable debris.

MATERIALS
- 2 10-by-8-inch (25.5-by-21-cm) pieces of paper
- Pen
- Scissors
- Small firesafe bowl
- 2 pinches forest dirt (for fear, nightmares)

- 1 valerian root (*Valeriana officinalis*) (for distressed sleep)
- 1 mandrake root (*Mandragora officinarum*) (for fear, nightmares)
- Herb grinder
- Spoon or wand
- Pin, needle, or knife
- Black taper candle
- Lighter or matches
- Candleholder
- Storage container
- Fire extinguisher or bowl of water

WORKING

1. Clear the outdoor work area of any debris, and set the fire extinguisher or bowl of water nearby.

2. Place one sheet of paper on top of the other, and use the pen to draw a human shape in the center of the paper. Use the scissors to cut out the shape, cutting through both pieces of paper.

3. On one figure write your target's name and date of birth. If that information is unknown, write words identifying your specific target. On the other figure, write what wrongs they have done. Set these pieces of paper aside.

4. Place the forest dirt in the bowl.

5. Grind both roots into a powderlike consistency. Add the ground roots to the bowl.

6. Mix the dirt and roots together. As you mix the materials, see your target having distressed sleep. See them having terrible nightmares. Direct the energy of those visualizations into the dirt.

7. Use the pin, needle, or knife to carve "Nightmares and Distressed Sleep" into two sides of the candle. Light the candle.

8. Hold the human-shaped pieces of paper together in one hand with the writing facing out. Use the wax melting from the candle to seal the figure. Seal all edges except for the head. Set the candle in the holder.

9. Pour the dirt and herb mixture into the poppet through the head. Once those materials have been added, use wax to seal the head.

10. Exhale into the poppet, giving it life, and name it for your target. After you name the poppet, state:

    For the pain you have caused me, a good sleep from you I do keep. When your lessons have been learned, from nightmares you will be free.

11. Place the poppet in the bowl, and use the candle to light the poppet on fire. Return the candle to the holder. As the poppet burns, know that your target will have nightmares until they stop harassing you or your loved ones.

12. Once the poppet has burned completely and is nothing but ash, extinguish the candle. Transfer the ash to the small container and close it.

13. Sprinkle the ash around a crossroads, knowing that your target will be attacked from all directions. Dispose of the candle in a trash can away from your home.

Rivers & Streams

Rivers and streams can be powerful magical locations. They share the properties of other bodies of water, such as purification, but because their waters move, they also contain the energy needed to attract things to or remove things from your life. The dirt from them is no different. When gathering dirt for your workings, use a compass to tell whether the water is flowing toward your home (attraction) or away from it (removal).

There are two other things to note when gathering river dirt. The first is that dirt from the riverbed is more powerful than dirt from the riverbank. Dirt from the bed is submerged within the moving water, while dirt from the bank is only grazed by the moving water. Second, you will usually need to wait for the dirt to dry before using it. When you first gather the dirt, it will be too muddy.

BRING NEW OPPORTUNITIES CHARM

This spell uses the power of river dirt to draw new opportunities into your life. It can be used for something specific, like changes in employment, or for general new opportunities.

MATERIALS

- Skeleton key (for opening doors)
- Small bowl
- ¼ cup (60 ml) river dirt (to attract opportunities)
- 1 foot (30.5 cm) necklace chain

WORKING

1. Place the skeleton key in the bowl. Sprinkle the dirt over the key. Cover as much of the key as possible. As you do so, recite the following chant five times:

   Dirt from a river flowing toward the sea,
   lend your power to open the doors for me.

2. Leave the key buried in the dirt for one week. Once a day hold your hands over the bowl and recite the previous chant five times, visualizing new opportunities coming your way.

3. After a week has passed, dig out the key and place it on the chain. Hang the chain on the inside of the door you use the most to enter and exit the house. Every time the door is used, the charm is activated and its energy sent out.

RIVER DIRT CRYSTAL CLEANSING SPELL

One common magical practice is to cleanse crystals and stones before use. Many people cleanse these crystals with water, not knowing that water damages those crystals. Other crystals can easily dissolve in water. To avoid harming these crystals, you can use the energy of river dirt to cleanse them instead.

While this spell is specifically designed for cleansing crystals, it can easily be adapted to work with any magical tool.

MATERIALS
- Crystal
- Small bowl
- ¼ cup (60 ml) river dirt (for cleansing, purification, removal)
- Storage container

WORKING
1. Place the crystal in the small bowl and cover the crystal with the river dirt.

2. Hold your hands over the covered crystal and state:

    Dirt from a river that flows free, cleanse this crystal of unwanted energy.

3. Visualize the dirt absorbing the unwanted energy from the crystal and taking that energy into itself. Keep the crystal covered for 24 hours.

4. After 24 hours, dig the crystal out of the dirt and dust it off. The crystal is now cleansed.

5. Keep the used dirt stored in the container until you can return to the river. When you do, put the dirt in the water. As the dirt moves with the river, the absorbed energy will move away as well.

TO CAUSE ONE TO BE BOGGED DOWN HEX

As with all forces in this world, river dirt can be used to cause harm and havoc in an individual's life.

This spell will trap an individual in their current life. No matter what they do, your target will be stuck, trapped in the river mud. To perform this spell, you will need access to a nearby stretch of river where you can be alone.

MATERIALS
- Pencil
- Unbleached 10-by-8-inch (25.5-by-21-cm) piece of paper
- Knife
- Large branch

WORKING
1. Write your target's name and date of birth on the piece of paper five times. Write each line underneath the one before. If your target's name is not known, write a few words identifying them.

2. Rotate the paper 90 degrees away from you, and repeat step 1, writing over the previous set of names and dates.

3. Carefully use the knife to sharpen one end of the large branch, leaving the other end as it was naturally. While you cut, direct all the anger, frustration, and annoyance you feel toward your target into the branch.

4. Take the branch and paper with you to the river. Find a place where you can leave both items, and use the branch to stab the paper into the river-bed. As you stab the paper, state:

> *May this river keep you in place. May you be lost and stuck without any trace.*

5. Walk away, leaving things as they are. Know your target will be trapped and unable to take any action to fix their life until you release them.

6. When you feel your target has learned their lesson, or you feel like releasing your target, remove the stick from the water and toss what remains of the paper into the trash, freeing your target from the immobilizing powers of the river mud. If a natural event, such as a storm or high wind, moves the stick and paper, it is safe to assume that your target has learned their lesson, and the spirit of the river freed them

Oceans & Coastal Beaches

My home state has miles of ocean beaches that are always full of life during the summer. Whenever I go to the beach, I can't help but feel like magic has been worked on me by the spirits of those locations. My soul always feels refreshed and renewed after time at the seaside.

Not all beaches are sandy. Some have rocks and dirt. All of the spells in this section are written using beach sand, but they work just as well with beach dirt. As with the river dirt, ocean sand or dirt usually needs to dry before use.

OCEAN BEACH POPPET CLEANSE SPELL

Ocean sand is a powerful cleansing force. In fact, its power comes from three different sources. The first source is the earth itself, which absorbs and neutralizes energetic forces. The second is the salt in the water, which can also be felt in the air. Salt also cleanses and neutralizes. The third source of cleansing energy is the ocean itself. Like all bodies of water, it has purifying powers.

The next time you are at the ocean, use this spell to cleanse yourself of any negativity and unwanted forces.

MATERIALS
- Beach pail
- Beach sand (for cleansing)
- Water from the ocean (for cleansing)
- Some of your hair, fingernails, or other personal effect, optional

WORKING
1. Gather the sand in the beach pail. If you are using a personal effect, add it to the pail while gathering the sand to effectively mix the two together.

2. Begin adding ocean water to the pail a little at a time until the dirt becomes a malleable mud.

3. Shape the mud into a vaguely human form. As you create the figure, direct your frustrations and the negativity you want removed from your life into it.

4. Exhale over the poppet to breathe life into the body and name it for yourself. State:

   Poppet, I name you (your name). As the sun dries you this day, all negativity within is sent away.

5. Set the poppet aside and let it dry. Return any remaining sand to the beach or ocean.

6. Once the poppet has dried, take the figure down to the water and destroy it. Let the energy within the figure be returned to the earth and feel yourself be cleansed.

Attract Sales & Customers Tidal Spell

The sea has long been a source of trade and income, and ocean sand can be a powerful tool when it comes to manifesting money and trade opportunities. When using ocean sand to attract something, be sure to use sand gathered when the tide was coming in.

Use this spell and the power of the tides to bring sales and customers to your business. This spell takes place in two parts, one at home and the other at the beach when the tide is turning from low to high. Be sure to look up your local tide schedule.

MATERIALS
- Pen
- 2 pieces of paper
- Stick of driftwood
- ¼ cup (60 ml) pine needles (*Pinus*) (for money, prosperity)

WORKING
1. On the first piece of paper, write out "Attract Sales and Loyal Customers." Then go through the words and cross out all of the repeated letters.

2. Still working on the first piece of paper, arrange the remaining letters into a design that you find appealing. As you create your design, focus on gaining new customers and increasing sales. Direct that energy into the symbol. The more time and effort you put into the design, the more powerful it will be.

3. When you have finished your design, copy it onto the second piece of paper.

4. Head to the beach when the tide is changing from low to high. Walk along the beach until you find a quiet spot where you will not be disturbed. As you walk, look for a small piece of driftwood.

5. Go to the water's edge and use the driftwood to draw the symbol you created. Focus on gaining new customers and an increase in sales.

6. Once the symbol is drawn, sprinkle the pine needles over it. As you sprinkle them, recite the following chant three to five times:

   Dirt of the ocean and sea, bring to me prosperity.

7. Walk away, leaving the driftwood there, and return to your daily life. The tide will take your message out to sea, sending your energy into the world freely.

TIDAL CHAOS CURSE

The tides are a very powerful force, and waves are often the strongest and most chaotic during the changing of the tides. This energy can be channeled and directed to bring chaos into someone's life.

Before performing this spell, be sure that you have not wronged your target in any way. If you have, your life will also become chaotic.

MATERIALS
- Pen
- 10-by-8-inch (25.5-by-21-cm) piece of paper
- Small storage container
- 3 tablespoons (45 ml) sand gathered when the tide was changing from low to high tide (for chaos)

- 3 tablespoons (45 ml) sand gathered when the tide was changing from high to low tide (for chaos)
- 2 tablespoons (30 ml) mustard seeds (*Brassica juncea*) (for chaos)
- 2 tablespoons (30 ml) poppy seeds (*Papaver somniferum*) (for confusion)

WORKING

1. On the paper, write the name and date of birth of your target. If their name or date of birth is unknown, write out some way that they can be clearly identified and targeted.

2. Place the paper in the container. Cover the paper with the dirt, then add the seeds.

3. Seal the container and shake it vigorously, directing all of your emotions regarding your target and their treatment of you or your loved ones into the container. While you shake, recite the following chant seven to nine times:

   Powers of the coastal tide, from your chaos we cannot hide. To (your target's name), chaos and confusion I do send, until their lesson they understand.

4. Place the container somewhere hidden in your home.

5. Once a day for the next month, shake the container and recite the same chant nine times to keep the spell activated.

6. After one month, go to the ocean and return the sand to release the spell. If your target has still not learned their lesson, continue the spell as before until they have.

Swamps

One of the more unique forms of earth is the swamp. Swamps are very magical places. They provide homes for a variety of plants and animals. Swamps are also great places for hiding things and being hidden. As with ocean and river dirt, dirt from a swamp should be dry before being used.

HIDE & PROTECT ME CHARM

Swamp dirt can be used to keep baneful attacks from reaching you or your loved ones. The negative energy will be lost in the swamp long before it ever comes near.

Use this spell to create an energetic barrier that will hide your energy from anyone who would wish you or your loved ones harm.

A small toy house taken from a board game will work best for this spell.

MATERIALS
- Image of a maze
- Small toy house
- Thorns from 1 rose (*Rosa*) (for protection)
- 2 pinches swamp dirt (to stay hidden)

WORKING

1. Place the house in the center of the maze.

2. Scatter the thorns over the maze. As you do so, state:

   To pierce evil sent this way. Baneful energy must not stay.

3. Sprinkle the swamp dirt around the maze. As you do so, see your energy and the energy of your loved ones being hidden in a maze of foggy energy. Know that baneful energy will not hit you at all. As you sprinkle the dirt, state:

   By the power of the swamp that hides me, from negativity I am free.

4. Once a week, sprinkle more dirt on the maze to keep the protection up. When you want to release the protection, dispose of the maze, thorns, and dirt in a trash can away from your home.

SWAMP UNDERWORLD PORTAL CHARM

Swamps possess an otherworldly energy, and realms like the underworld often feel much closer when a person is visiting a swamp. This association provides powerful magic for protection and spirit work. This spell works with swamp dirt to create a door and pathway to the underworld. When holding this charm, you can travel to the spirit world with ease.

MATERIALS

- Small plate
- Skeleton key (to open doors to the underworld)
- 3 tablespoons (45 ml) swamp dirt (as an underworld portal)
- 1 teaspoon (5 ml) basil (*Ocimum basilicum*) (to attract spirits and for underworld work)
- 1 teaspoon (5 ml) mugwort (*Artemisia vulgaris*) (for psychic and spirit sight)
- 1 teaspoon (5 ml) parsley (*Petroselinum crispum*) (for underworld work)
- 1 teaspoon (5 ml) wormwood (*Artemisia absinthium*) (for underworld work, protection while in the underworld)

WORKING

1. Place the skeleton key on the plate.

2. Cover the key with the swamp dirt. As you cover the key, state:

    Key that has no true door, you shall open the path to the underworld now and forever more.

3. Sprinkle the basil over the swamp dirt. State:

    Basil for the dead and gone that we may get along.

4. Lay the mugwort over and around the swamp dirt. State:

    Mugwort for psychic sight, that I might see the spirits from the rite.

5. Sprinkle the parsley over the dirt. State:

   Herb of parsley, to the underworld you are a key.

6. Sprinkle the wormwood over the dirt. State:

   Herb of spirit sight, help me travel to the underworld with your might.

7. Leave the key buried under the herbs and dirt for 24 hours. After 24 hours, the key will be charged. Dispose of the herbs and dirt by returning the items to the earth in some way.

8. Whenever you are ready to perform underworld meditations or trance work, hold the key. It will work as a charm to activate and open underworld doors.

9. To keep the charm charged, repeat the burying process on a new or dark moon.

TO BRING FEAR & HORROR CURSE

Swamps are often considered creepy and scary. Just think about all the horror movies and scary stories that take place in swampy locations. This association makes dirt from swampy locations perfect for baneful magic.

Use this spell when you need to make someone feel afraid for a short period of time. While the candle burns, your target will know fear.

MATERIALS

- Pin, needle, or knife
- Black skull candle
- Small plate
- 3 pinches swamp dirt (for baneful magic, fear)
- 1 pinch crushed fire ants (for baneful magic, fear)
- 2 pinches wormwood (*Artemisia absinthium*) (for fear)
- Lighter or matches

WORKING

1. Use the pin, needle, or knife to carve the name of your target into the candle.

2. Place the candle on the small plate.

3. Sprinkle the dirt, ants, and wormwood around the base of the candle.

4. Light the candle, stating:

   As this candle does burn, to feel fear now is your turn.

5. Let the candle burn out.

6. Once the candle is done burning and the wax has cooled, dispose of the materials in a trash can away from your home. If you cannot burn the candle in one sitting, burn the candle for 5 to 10 minutes a day until it's gone, then dispose of the materials.

Deserts

Deserts are harsh environments, and the plants and animals that call deserts home need strength to survive and persist in the difficult conditions.

STRENGTH TO PULL THROUGH SPELL

This spell helps you call on your inner strength when you are going through a difficult time. Use it to help you see the solution to your problem and manifest the energy to work through it.

MATERIALS
- Old, worn sock (as a personal effect)
- Scissors
- 3 tablespoons (45 ml) desert sand (for strength)
- 1 tablespoon (15 ml) woodruff (*Galium odoratum*) (for courage, strength)
- 1 tablespoon (15 ml) plantain (*Plantago major*) leaf (for courage, strength)
- 1 foot (30.5 cm) black thread
- Needle

WORKING
1. Cut the toe section from the sock and toss the rest of the sock away.

2. Fill the toe area with the desert sand and herbs.

3. Thread the needle, and stitch the open end of the sock closed, reciting the following chant until you've finished:

Desert sand, powerful and strong, help me find the strength I've had all along.

4. Carry the packet with you every day as you face problems and come to solutions. Know that you have the strength and courage within to face every problem that comes your way.

5. When you have overcome your problems, dispose of the packet in a trash can far from your home.

I NEED CASH NOW SPELL

During the day, desert sand can get quite hot. This heat can be used to add speed to your magic and generate quick results.

Use this spell to bring cash to you quickly. For this working, it is best to have a specific need for the cash, like bill payment, class registration, etc.

The recipe for fast-money powder can be found in part 3.

MATERIALS
- Small bowl
- Spoon or wand
- 3 tablespoons (45 ml) desert sand (for quick results)
- 3 tablespoons (45 ml) fast-money powder
- Your wallet
- Your daily shoes

WORKING

1. In the bowl, use the spoon or wand to mix the desert sand and the powder thoroughly. As you mix the materials, recite:

   Desert sand, full of speed, bring to me the money I need.

2. Sprinkle some of the mixture inside your wallet. State:

   To attract money quick, that is the trick.

3. Sprinkle the rest of the mixture in your shoes, reciting the following chant three to five times:

   Every step I take each day, attracts money my way.

4. Every morning before you head out for the day, hold your hands over your shoes and recite the previous chant five times. Continue this daily work until you have all the cash you need.

BURY THE PAST & MOVE ON HEALING SPELL

Deserts are mostly barren landscapes with relatively little plant and animal life. This makes desert dirt excellent for banishing and baneful magic. Use this spell to leave the past in the past.

This is a two-part spell involving a cut-and-clear followed by a removal. Before performing it, be sure you are completely done with whatever you wish to banish. If there are any lingering connections, this spell will not work. It will bring you harm instead of a healing release.

MATERIALS
- Pen
- 10-by-8-inch (25.5-by-21-cm) piece of paper
- 2 feet (61 cm) black ribbon
- Scissors
- Small storage container
- ¼ cup (60 ml) desert sand (for banishing)

WORKING
1. On the paper, write out what you wish to banish from your life.

2. Roll the paper into a small scroll, rolling away from you, and bind it with the ribbon. As you bind the scroll, state:

   From my past, I am free. A new start for me.

3. Place the paper in the small container. Cover the paper with the desert sand. As you do so, recite the following chant five to seven times:

   From my past, I am free at last.

4. Once the paper is covered, seal the container and shake it vigorously, directing all of your anger, frustrations, and other negative feelings into the container. Feel yourself being freed from these negative sensations. While you shake, recite the chant from step 4 five to seven times.

5. For one month, keep the container in a dark place—out of sight and mind. At the end of the month, take the container to a trash can far from your home and dispose of it. Turn your back to the trash can and return home, free from your past.

BUSINESSES, PUBLIC
SERVICES & MORE

B usinesses and public services are urban locations. Like
natural locations, each urban location has a spirit and
force, and it is just as important to develop relationships
with them. In fact, the same process you used to develop
relationships with natural locations can be used to develop
relationships with urban ones.

Public service locations are those that provide some sort
of service for the public. Some of these locations are owned
by the public (e.g., public schools and libraries). Other locations, such as banks and hospitals, are privately owned.

Public service locations gain their energy from the
actions that occur there. The more an action is repeated
at a location, the more energy the location will absorb. By
taking a look at the actions and activities that take place at a

specific location, you can figure out the location's energetic correspondences.

Something to keep in mind is that these locations usually have lots of people going in and out of them. For best results, try to visit these locations during times when there is not as much traffic. This may mean going early in the morning, just as places open up, or late at night, when things are closing down. With less human activity, it will be easier to contact and connect with the spirits of the land. It will be easier to gather the dirt you need without being noticed or observed too.

Church & Temple Dirt

Dirt harvested from a church or temple is a very unique item. Churches and temples are the homes of the deities or spirits that are honored or worshipped there. All prayers or rituals worked at these locations empower the dirt with the essence and power of the deities.

CALL ON YOUR GOD BLESSING

Use this working to create a powder charged with the essence of a deity. Anytime you want to add their power to a spell, simply incorporate a pinch of this mixture into the work.

As written, this spell focuses on Christianity. To modify this spell to work with a different deity, use herbs and a symbol that are sacred to the deity and recite a prayer for them.

MATERIALS

- Small bowl
- Spoon or wand
- 1 tablespoon (15 ml) churchyard dirt (for divine energy)
- 1 tablespoon (15 ml) ground or powdered frankincense (*Boswellia sacra*) (sacred to Yahweh)
- 1 tablespoon (15 ml) basil (*Ocimum basilicum*) (sacred to Yahweh)
- 1 tablespoon (15 ml) ground myrrh (*Commiphora myrrha*) (sacred to Jesus)
- Small storage container
- Pen and label sticker

WORKING

1. In the bowl, mix the dirt and herbal materials together. As you stir, recite the Lord's Prayer nine times, feeling the mixture fill up with the holy power of God:

   > *Our Father in heaven,*
   > *hallowed be your name.*
   > *your kingdom come,*
   > *your will be done,*
   > *on earth as it is in heaven.*
   > *Give us today our daily bread.*
   > *And forgive us our debts,*
   > *as we have also forgiven our debtors.*
   > *And lead us not into temptation,*
   > *but deliver us from the evil one.*[8]

---

8. "Matthew 6:9–13 (New International Version)," Bible Gateway.

2. Hold your hands over the bowl. State:

   In the name of the Father, the Son, and the Holy Spirit, the Sacred Trinity, I charge and bless this holy blend. Lend your power and blessings to this dirt. In your name, I pray.

3. Keep your hands over the bowl until you feel the contents pulsating with strong sacred energy.

4. Draw a cross over the bowl with your dominant hand to seal in the energy.

5. Pour the mixture into the container. Label the container "God's Blessing Powder," and store it with your other herbal mixes and powders. Whenever you need to add the power of Yahweh to your work, add a pinch of this mixture.

GOD'S HEALING SPELL

When it comes to prayers offered to the Divine, prayers related to healing are among those most commonly made. For this reason, dirt from a church or temple can be a powerful ingredient in healing spells.

Use church or temple dirt in this spell to sending healing energy to a loved one. As always, make sure you have the individual's permission to work magic on their behalf.

The recipe for healing anointing oil can be found in part 3.

MATERIALS

- Photo or image of the target
- Pen
- Pin, needle, or knife
- Blue or white taper candle
- Healing anointing oil
- Small plate
- Taper candleholder
- 1 tablespoon (15 ml) churchyard dirt (for healing)
- 1 tablespoon (15 ml) allheal (*Prunella vulgaris*) (for healing)
- 1 tablespoon (15 ml) marigold (*Calendula officinalis*) (for healing)
- 1 tablespoon (15 ml) oregano (*Origanum vulgare*) (for healing)
- 1 tablespoon (15 ml) lemon balm (*Melissa officinalis*) (for healing)
- Zest from 1 lime (*Citrus × aurantiifolia*) (for cleansing, removal)
- 1 teaspoon (5 ml) mace (*Myristica fragrans*) (for protection, removal)

WORKING

1. On the back of the photo, write your target's name and date of birth. If you know the specifics of the healing needed, write those details under their name and date of birth. If those specifics aren't known, write "General Healing" under their name and date of birth instead.

2. Use the pin, needle, or knife to carve the symbol for Mercury into one side of the candle. On the

other side, carve the name of the individual who needs healing.

☿

3. Anoint the candle from the center out with the oil. As you rub the candle with the oil, state:

   Healing for (name) on this day.

4. Place the photo face up on the plate and set the candleholder on top of the photo. Set the candle in the holder and light it.

5. Sprinkle the church dirt around the candle on the plate. As you sprinkle the dirt, recite Psalm 6:2 five times:

   Have mercy on me, Lord, for I am faint;
   heal me, Lord, for my bones are in agony.[9]

6. Sprinkle each of the herbs one at a time around the candle and over the photo. As you sprinkle each herb, state what it is being used for, then recite Jeremiah 33:6:

   Nevertheless, I will bring health and heal-
   ing to it; I will heal my people and will let
   them enjoy abundant peace and security.[10]

7. Let the candle burn out completely. If you are unable to burn the entire candle in one sitting,

---

9. "Psalm 6:2 (New International Version)," BibleGateway.
10. "Jeremiah 33:6 (New International Version)," BibleGateway.

burn the candle for 10 minutes daily until it is completely burned. Each time the candle is lit, recite Psalm 6:2 three times.

8. Once the candle has burned out completely, dispose of the materials. If possible, bury the herbs and dirt in the earth around the home of your target. Otherwise, dispose of the materials in the trash near your home.

Medical Spaces

When it comes to healing magic, there is no better location to work with than hospitals and the offices of medical professionals. These locations are places of life and death. They hold the powers of healing and curing as well as destruction and death.

Remember that no magic is an appropriate substitute for medical treatment. Always seek proper medical treatment before performing any specific form of healing magic.

PROMOTE HEALING PACKET SPELL

Sometimes colds and illnesses take longer to get over than we would like. Use this spell to boost the healing of your body and mind.

If you are dealing with any chronic illnesses, know that this spell is for working through a current flair up or bout, not curing the illness itself.

MATERIALS

- Pen
- Paper
- Personal effect
- 2 pinches hospital or doctor's office dirt (for healing)
- 1 teaspoon (5 ml) marigold (*Calendula officinalis*) (for healing)
- 1 teaspoon (5 ml) lavender (*Lavandula angustifolia*) (for healing)
- 1 teaspoon (5 ml) ginkgo leaf (*Ginkgo biloba*) (for healing)
- 1 foot (30.5 cm) blue ribbon

WORKING

1. On the paper, write out the illnesses or issues you need help healing.

2. Place the personal effect on top of the petition.

3. Sprinkle the hospital dirt across the personal effect.

4. Add the herbs to the paper in any order, stating that they be used to boost healing.

5. Fold the paper in half toward you three times. As you fold, chant:

   Strength today. Healing energy stay.

6. Wrap the blue ribbon around the packet three times, reciting the chant from step 5. Tie a knot to seal in the healing energy.

7. Carry the charm with you as long as you need the healing boost. If you made the charm for another person, give it to them to carry. When the healing is no longer needed, dispose of the packet in a trash can somewhere outside of the home.

Protect against Illness Sachet

This spell helps create an energetic ward against illnesses. Use it when you feel yourself starting to get run down or at the beginning of cold/flu season.

MATERIALS
- Blue drawstring bag
- Personal effect
- 3 pinches hospital or doctor's office dirt (for healing)
- 1 tablespoon (15 ml) ground horseradish root (*Armoracia rusticana*) (for banishment, purification)
- 1 tablespoon (15 ml) ground black peppercorn (*Piper nigrum*) (for protection, removal)
- 1 tablespoon (15 ml) lavender (*Lavandula angustifolia*) (for healing)
- 1 tablespoon (15 ml) lemon zest (*Citrus × limon*)
- 1 tablespoon (15 ml) lemon balm (*Melissa officinalis*) (for healing)
- Small quartz tumble (to empower all other materials)
- 3 to 5 drops eucalyptus essential oil (*Eucalyptus*) (for cleansing, healing)

- 3 to 5 drops tea tree essential oil (*Melaleuca alternifolia*) (for protection, reversal)

WORKING

1. Place the personal effect in the drawstring bag. State:

   > *Protect me (or name of individual in need of healing) from illness.*

2. Sprinkle the dirt into the pouch. As you sprinkle the dirt, state:

   > *With the power of modern medicine, against illnesses I (they) win.*

3. Add the herbs to the pouch in any order, stating why each herb is being used.

4. Place the quartz tumble in the bag. State:

   > *Empower today the herbs to keep illnesses away.*

5. Pull the bag closed, and anoint it with the eucalyptus oil, stating:

   > *Cleanse and clean away the negative and illness this day.*

6. Anoint the bag with the tea tree oil, stating:

   > *Protection from the sick. Send it back with a kick.*

7. Carry the charm with you as long as you feel the need for the boost in protection. If the charm is for someone else, give it to them. Once a week, anoint the charm with the two essential oils.

8. Dispose of the charm when you no longer feel the need for its protection. Create a new charm as needed. For best results, make one each cold/flu season.

Mental Health Distress Hex

Some medical facilities focus on a specific ailment or body part, and harvesting dirt from a specialist's office allows you to target needs related to that speciality. For example, dirt from a dentist's office can be used for dental needs, while dirt harvested from an optometrist's office can be used for eye issues.

This spell uses dirt from a behavioral health clinic or psychologist's office to target someone who doesn't understand what living with mental illness is like and makes cruel and hurtful comments as a result. They may constantly gaslight or make fun of people struggling with mental illnesses. The goal of the spell is to make them live with such distress until they understand what it's like to experience it and change their ways.

When performing this spell, wear sturdy shoes like boots or sneakers.

MATERIALS
- Knife
- Whole mandrake root (*Mandragora officinarum*) (for curses, mental distress, nightmares)
- 1 pinch dirt from a mental health center (to cause mental distress)

- 1 tablespoon (15 ml) ground poppy seeds (*Papaver somniferum*) (for confusion)
- 1 pin for each stress or issue you want your target to have

WORKING

1. Use the knife to carve your target's name into the mandrake root. If their name is not known, carve the words "My Target," and picture your target in your mind as you carve them.

2. Rub the dirt and poppy seeds into the words you carved.

3. Stab each pin into the mandrake root. As you do so, state what stress or issue that pin represents.

4. Place the mandrake root on the floor and stomp on it. Grind the anger and frustrations you have for the target into the root.

5. Once daily for a month, stomp on the mandrake root, directing the energy toward your target.

6. When you feel your target has learned their lesson, remove the pins from the root, and toss the root and pins in the trash. The spell has been released.

Banks & Other Financial Institutions

Dirt harvested from banks and financial institutions can be used in any workings related to money or finances. From fast cash to landing loans and protecting your money, bank dirt is your tool. Any way that you can connect with that bank energy can be used to work money magic.

ATTRACT MONEY PACKET SPELL

This is a generic spell to attract money. I use this spell when I just need a little extra spending money.

MATERIALS
- Small magnet (for attraction)
- Dollar bill
- 1 pinch bank dirt (for finances and money)

WORKING
1. Place the magnet in the center of the dollar bill.

2. Sprinkle the bank dirt over the magnet, stating:

   Dirt from a bank with money, bring me cash sweet as honey.

3. Fold the dollar bill over the magnet, folding toward you to attract money. Continue to fold the dollar bill until you have a small packet that can fit in your pocket or wallet.

4. Carry the packet with you, allowing it to draw money your way.

5. When you no longer need the extra cash, return the dirt to the earth. Hold on to the magnet for use in other magical works. Spend the dollar bill at a store you frequent to spread the blessings.

PROTECT MY MONEY JAR SPELL

Use this spell to protect your income and ensure that you always have the financial means to live your life. This spell protects against unexpected expenses and financial emergencies.

MATERIALS
- Coins and cash
- Small mason jar with lid
- 1 teaspoon (5 ml) bank dirt (for protection of money)
- 1 tablespoon (15 ml) marigold flowers (*Calendula officinalis*) (for luck, money, protection of your money, success)
- 1 tablespoon (15 ml) sunflower seeds (*Helianthus annuus*) (for prosperity, success)
- Tiger's-eye tumble (for protection of money)

WORKING
1. Place the coins and cash in the jar.

2. Sprinkle the bank dirt over the money and state:

   Protect my money for me. From financial stress, I am free.

3. Add the marigold flowers and sunflower seeds. Recite the statement from step 2 as you add them.

4. Place the tiger's-eye tumble in the jar. Repeat the same statement.

5. Seal the jar, and shake it vigorously. While you shake the jar, visualize a shield or safe protecting you and all of your money. Direct that image into the jar. As you shake the jar and hold the visualization, chant the following statement seven to nine times:

   Protect my money for me. From financial stress, I am free.

6. Place the jar on a shelf where it won't be disturbed.

7. Twice a day shake the jar, reciting the same chant as before. The spell will remain active as long as you continue to shake the jar regularly.

8. When you no longer need the extra protection, deposit the cash into your account. Dispose of the herbs in the trash or compost. The jar and tumble can be cleansed and used in future magical works.

SWEETEN LOAN APPLICATION PACKET SPELL

Use this spell before you apply for a loan. The goal of this spell is to increase the odds of your application being approved.

MATERIALS
- Bank envelope
- Pen

- Slip of paper
- 1 pinch bank dirt (for finances, money)
- 1 pinch rosemary (*Salvia rosmarinus*) (to open one's mind)
- 2 pinches sugar (for sweetening)
- 2 pinches masterwort (*Astrantia major*) (for domination)
- 1 pinch lavender (*Lavandula angustifolia*) (for mental focus, sweetening)
- 1 pinch chamomile (*Matricaria recutita*) (for mind, money, sweetening)

WORKING

1. On the outside of the envelope, write out what type of loan you are trying to get in capital letters.

2. On the paper, write out a petition explaining why you need the money and about how much money you need. Fold the petition in half and place it in the envelope.

3. Add the bank dirt to the envelope.

4. Place each of the remaining materials in the envelope, stating why you are using each one as you do so.

5. Seal the envelope and shake it. As you work the envelope, chant:

   A loan for me. A blessed future I see.

6. Carry the envelope with you every day until you apply for the loan. At least once a day, shake the

envelope and recite the same chant three to five times.

7. When you apply for the loan, have the envelope on you.

8. If you land the loan, dispose of the envelope in a trash can within the bank. If you do not get the loan, toss the packet into a trash can outside and away from the bank. Wait a while before you try again. When you are ready to apply again, create a new packet.

Courthouse Dirt

Courts are places to seek justice as well as protection. Use the following spells to protect yourself from harm and bring forth justice. The dirt used in these spells can come from anywhere in the courthouse. Getting dirt from the courtroom itself is ideal, but when that is not possible, any dirt from the courthouse will work.

KEEP ABUSE AWAY POWDER

Use this spell when you are trying to get away from abuse or are otherwise in danger. The goal of this spell is to prevent the abuser from finding you and continuing their abuse.

This spell involves burning paper. For safety, perform this spell outside in an area cleared of debris. Have a fire extinguisher or bowl of water nearby.

MATERIALS

- Bowl of water or fire extinguisher
- Pen
- Paper
- Scissors
- Firesafe bowl
- Lighter or matches
- 1 tablespoon (15 ml) courthouse dirt (for protection from abuse)
- 1 teaspoon (5 ml) ground black peppercorn (*Piper nigrum*) (for protection)
- 1 teaspoon (5 ml) angelica root (*Angelica archangelica*) (for protection)
- 1 teaspoon (5 ml) ginger (*Zingiber officinale*) (for justice, protection)
- Spoon or wand
- Storage container
- Label sticker

WORKING

1. Clear your outdoor work area of any debris, and place the fire extinguisher or bowl of water nearby.

2. On the paper, write the name of the person who is abusing you. Under their name, write out how they are abusing you. Once everything is written down, draw a huge "X" over the words to symbolize no more abuse.

3. Cut the paper into small pieces. Place the pieces in the firesafe bowl.

4. Set the paper on fire. As the paper burns, feel yourself being protected. Know that the person who's been harming you will stay away.

5. Once the fire has died out and the ash has cooled, add the dirt and herbal materials to the bowl.

6. Use the spoon or wand to mix the ash, dirt, and herbs together. As you stir, recite the following chant seven to nine times:

   Abuser be gone. Let my life move along.

7. Pour the mix into the storage container. Label the container "Abuse Keep Away Powder."

8. Once a week (or more if needed), sprinkle the mixture across your front door for protection from your abuser and to keep them away. Create more of the powder as needed. When you no longer need the protection, dispose of any remaining mixture away from your home.

PEACEFUL & JUST SEPARATION WORKING

This spell can be performed when you or a loved one is experiencing a divorce or separation. You can also use this spell when long-term relationships that were not legally bound are ending. The goal of the spell is to make sure the relationship ends peacefully, without either side hurting or taking advantage of the other.

MATERIALS

- Two white candles
- Pin, needle, or knife
- 2 candleholders
- 2 feet (61 cm) cooking twine
- Small bowl
- Spoon or wand
- 1 teaspoon (5 ml) courthouse dirt (for peaceful separation)
- 2 tablespoons (30 ml) rosemary (*Salvia rosmarinus*) (for family, household)
- 2 tablespoons (30 ml) lavender (*Lavandula angustifolia*) (for peace)
- 2 tablespoons (30 ml) chamomile (*Matricaria recutita*) (for peace)
- 4 rose thorns (*Rosa*) (for protection of emotions)
- Lighter or matches
- Scissors

WORKING

1. Use the pin, needle, or knife to carve the name of one of the individuals into a candle. Carve the name of the second person into the other candle.

2. Place the candles in their holders.

3. Tie the twine to the candleholders. One end of twine should be tied to one holder and the other end tied to the other holder.

4. In the bowl, mix the dirt and herbal materials together. While you stir, visualize the relationship dissolving peacefully. See the two parties

ending things on good terms and remaining civil. Hold that imagery for as long as you can. When you can no longer hold on to the visualization, direct all of the imagery and mental energy into the materials in the bowl.

5. Move the candles away from one another until the twine is taut. Light the candles.

6. Sprinkle the herb and dirt mixture around the two candles. Make one large circle that encompasses both candles. As you sprinkle, state:

> *Relationship between (targets' names), dissolve peacefully. Let there be no pain or strife between thee.*

7. Continue sprinkling and reciting until there is a complete circle of the mixture around the candles.

8. Let the candles burn for about 5 minutes. Hold the scissors over the twine and state:

> *It's time for you two to part ways. I cut the ties that bind today.*

9. Cut the twine.

10. Gently push the candles slightly farther away from one another. As you move the candles, state:

> *From this relationship, you are free. Happier going forward you both shall be.*

11. Let the candles burn out completely. When the candles have stopped burning, dispose of them

in a trash can somewhere your targets won't find them.

Schools, Libraries & Training Centers

Libraries and education and training facilities provide access to all sorts of knowledge. Libraries are full of books, and they also have computers that people can use to apply for any assistance they may need. Colleges, trade schools, and universities offer training and knowledge for a variety of careers and fields of expertise. When it comes to magical work, the dirt from these locations can be used to enhance studies and open the doors to new opportunities.

STUDY AID PACKET

Use this spell to boost your memory when studying for a test or exam.

The spell will not replace studying or practicing any necessary skills; it only works as a booster to help you remember what you need for the test.

MATERIALS
- Paper
- Pen
- 1 teaspoon (5 ml) ginkgo leaf (*Ginkgo biloba*) (for focus, mental processes)
- 1 teaspoon (5 ml) rosemary (*Salvia rosmarinus*) (for memory, mental processes)

- 1 teaspoon (5 ml) dirt from where the test will occur (to fight test anxiety and for education, memory)

WORKING

1. On the paper, write out what you are studying and what you need to focus on for the upcoming exam.

2. Sprinkle the ginkgo leaf over what you just wrote and state:

   For focus and concentration.

3. Sprinkle the rosemary over the ginkgo leaf and state:

   To remember what I need for my exam.

4. Add the dirt. State:

   For memory, concentration, and focus. May you help me remember all that I study today.

5. Fold the paper in half. State:

   As my studies fill my mind, come exam time, all the answers I will find.

6. Rotate the paper and repeat the fold and statement. Do this three more times.

7. Hold your hands over the folded packet and visualize yourself passing the exam and knowing the answer to every question asked. Hold the image for as long as you can. When you can no longer hold the visualization, release the image and the energy into the packet.

8. Keep the packet with you while you study. Every so often as you study and find something you have difficulty with, play with the packet.

9. Carry the packet in your pocket or purse on the day of the exam. During the exam, play with the packet as needed until you finish the exam.

10. After the exam, dispose of the packet in the trash and walk away confident that you passed the test.

OBTAIN NEW SKILLS TALISMAN

This spell is to help you acquire the training necessary to enhance your employment opportunities. You can use this spell when you have been unable to find training opportunities or to simply open the door to them.

MATERIALS
- Mixing bowl
- 2 tablespoons (30 ml) library or training center dirt (for learning new skills)
- 1 tablespoon (15 ml) basil (*Ocimum basilicum*) (for door opening)
- 1 tablespoon (15 ml) pine needles (*Pinus*) (for cleansing, prosperity, success)
- Mixing bowl
- Spoon or wand
- Skeleton key (to open doors)
- Key chain ring
- Small storage container
- Pen and label sticker

WORKING

1. Put the dirt in the bowl. As you add the dirt, state:

   For new skills and opportunities.

2. Add the basil and state:

   To open the door for new opportunities and more.

3. Sprinkle the pine needles into the bowl, stating:

   To cleanse all blocks and bring prosperity and success.

4. Mix the herbs and dirt thoroughly. While you mix the materials, visualize a door in front of you being unlocked and flung open. From that door, visualize yourself walking down a path filled with new skills and opportunities. See yourself obtaining degrees or certifications of training. Direct that energy down your arms, through your hands, and through the spoon or wand into the mixture. Maintain the images and energy exchange as long as you can. When you can no longer hold on to the imagery, release the energy down your arms, through your hands, and into the mixture.

5. Place the skeleton key in the bowl. If possible, bury the skeleton key in the mixture. You want the key to be in contact with as much of the mixture as possible. While covering the key, state:

   Key that opens the way, unlock all locked doors this day. Let training and new skills come my way.

6. Hold your hands over the bowl. Visualize a locked door being forced open by a light in the shape of the key. Direct all of that energy into the bowl and the key. Hold that image for as long as you can. When you can no longer hold the visualization, release the energy into the key.

7. Remove the key from the mixture and attach it to the key ring.

8. Carry the new key chain with you as long as you feel the need for doors to be opened. As long as you carry the key chain with you, you will have opportunities to learn new skills.

9. Pour the remaining mixture into the storage container. Label it "Door Opening Powder." Set this mixture aside and use it to recharge the key as needed. To recharge the key, sprinkle a little of the mixture over it, visualizing doors opening to new skills and opportunities.

10. When you no longer need these specific doors opened, remove the key from the key chain and bury it in salt to cleanse it for use in other workings. Toss the remaining mixture in a trash can.

Transportation Centers & Shipping Centers

When you work magic, you are working to create a change in your life. You are either trying to attract or remove something from your life, and dirt harvested from any place where people or materials are transported from one location to another can be used in these works.

Before cars and planes, trains were the primary method of moving people and goods across the United States. Train track dirt is the most traditional form of transportation dirt, but dirt from bus stations, airports, and postal or mailing services can be used just as effectively.

If you want to work with the dirt from train tracks, watch the trains that travel by your home. If the trains move toward your home, use the dirt to attract things into your life. If the trains move away from your home, use the dirt to remove things from your life.

ATTRACT BUSINESS BALL CHARM

For many online shops, it can be hard to gain the attention of customers outside of their immediate contact lists. This spell is designed to help attract customers from all over to your small business.

MATERIALS
- Clear plastic ornament ball
- 7 tablespoons (105 ml) transportation dirt (for attraction and to bring to you)
- 1 tablespoon (15 ml) gold stone chips (for money)
- 1 tablespoon (15 ml) basil (*Ocimum basilicum*) (to attract money and for protection, wealth)
- 1 tablespoon (15 ml) cinquefoil (*Potentilla simplex*) (to attract money)

- 1 tablespoon (15 ml) marigold (*Calendula officinalis*) (to protect money)
- 1 tablespoon (15 ml) aventurine chips (to attract money and sales)
- 1 tablespoon (15 ml) sugar (for attraction, money, sweetness)
- Superglue

WORKING

1. Place a tablespoon of the transportation dirt in the ball. State:

   To attract customers near and far.

2. Begin to layer the remaining materials, starting with the gold stone. As you add each layer, state why you are using that material. After each new material, add a tablespoon of the transportation dirt. The top layer should be the last tablespoon of transportation dirt.

3. Hold the ball and direct a gold and green light into it to charge it with sales and financial growth. Hold an image in your mind of your business growing and your sales increasing. When you can no longer hold that image, release that energy into the ball.

4. Carefully line the inside of the ball's cover with glue and seal the ball. Set it aside to dry.

5. Place the charm wherever you receive orders or service requests. You can also keep it near a cash register if your business uses one.

6. Once a week, hold the ball and repeat step 3. Continue this process as long as you need the extra sales boost.

7. When you are ready to end the spell, toss the decorative ball into the trash away from your home or place of work.

ATTRACT A PLACE OF EMPLOYMENT SPELL

Sometimes there are companies that we would like to work for that are not within our area. Instead of relocating for the work, you can use the dirt from a transportation center to draw those businesses to your area and thus attract yourself employment.

MATERIALS
- Small plate
- 2 business cards or ads for the company you want to work for
- Magnet (for attraction)
- 2 pinches transportation center dirt (for attraction)
- Iron pyrite or gold stone tumble (for money, wealth)
- 2 tablespoons (30 ml) sugar (for attraction, wealth)

WORKING
1. Place one of the businesses cards or ads in the center of the plate.

2. Set the magnet in the center of the business card or ad. State:

   To attract (name of business) to (name of your town/region).

3. Sprinkle the dirt over the magnet. State:

   (Name of business) far away, come to (town/region) to stay. From you do I wish to be paid.

4. Place the iron pyrite or gold stone in the center of the magnet, on top of business card. State:

   To be in (company's name)'s employ would be a great joy.

5. Set the second business card or ad on top of the stone.

6. Sprinkle the sugar around the magnet and business card sandwich.

7. Set the plate somewhere it won't be distributed and leave it alone. Over time, you will hear news of your target business opening up in your area. When that occurs, apply for the position you desire. Only dispose of or discard the sugar after you have secured employment. The stone and magnets can be cleansed and used in other magical projects.

Stop Signs

The main thing stop sign dirt is used for is causing things to stop. Every time a car reaches such a sign, it has to stop, and the dirt there contains the energy from every one of those stops. You can use the dirt harvested from these spots to create a short pause, create obstacles, and even prevent things from happening.

STOP & PROTECT AGAINST GOSSIP SACHET

Stop sign dirt can be used to put a hold on all sorts of things, but one of the most common uses is to put an end to gossip.

This spell is a modified version of the charm I created for a friend who was being targeted by gossip at work. Use this spell to protect yourself or friends from the influence of gossip.

MATERIALS
- 2 pieces of devil's shoestring (*Viburnum alnifolium*) (for ensnaring evil)
- 2 small mirrors (for reversal and to reflect back and return to sender)
- 2 feet (61 cm) black ribbon
- Black drawstring pouch
- 3 tablespoons (45 ml) stop sign dirt (to cause a behavior to stop)
- 1 tablespoon (15 ml) galangal (*Alpinia galanga*) root (for justice upon gossipers)
- Small tiger's-eye tumble (for protection against gossip)

WORKING
1. Place the two pieces of devil's shoestring together in the shape of a cross.

2. Set the devil's shoestring between the two mirrors. The reflective surfaces should be facing each other.

3. Wrap the mirror bundle with the ribbon. As you wrap the bundle, repeat the following chant until it is completely covered.

   The price of gossip is never free. Ensnared by its trap, you shall be.

4. Once the bundle is completely covered, tie a knot and place the bundle in the pouch.

5. Sprinkle the stop sign dirt over the bundle in the pouch and state:

   Stop gossip's spread. The truth rises instead.

6. Add the galangal root to the bag. State:

   To bring justice to those who gossip.

7. Place the tiger's-eye in the bag. State:

   To protect (your name or the name of the person you are making this sachet for) against gossip. May their words have no harm.

8. If you made the sachet for yourself, carry it with you whenever you are going to be around the people you suspect are gossiping. If you made the charm for another person, give it to them and instruct them to carry it with them in the same fashion you would.

9. Once the gossip has stopped, dispose of the sachet in a trash can away from the community or workspace the gossip occurred at and go about your day.

PROTECTION AGAINST UNRULY CUSTOMERS SPELL

Some customers just create problems. Use this spell to stop or prevent any customers from making any negative or disparaging comments against you.

MATERIALS
- Black pen
- Paper
- Scissors
- Small bowl
- 1 pinch dirt from your work (as a connection to your place of work)
- 1 pinch stop sign dirt (to stop disparaging comments)
- Red pen
- 3 pins

WORKING
1. On the paper, draw a rough human shape. In the center of the figure, write "Unruly Customers."

2. Use the scissors to cut the human shape out.

3. Sprinkle the dirt from your work over the figure. State:

   To protect (workplace) from unruly customers.

4. Sprinkle the stop sign dirt over the figure. State:

   To stop customers from causing issues.

5. Use the red pen to draw a mouth on the figure. Draw three red "X"s across the mouth you just drew.

6. Stick one pin in each red "X." As you stick each pin, state:

   Problematic customer of the day, nothing bad can you say.

7. The next time you go into work, dispose of the figure and materials in the trash.

SOCIAL SPACES

Wherever people gather, there is going to be the release and transfer of energy, and when it comes to social spaces, there is a substantial field of energy for you to work with. The more people interacting and socializing, the more power the location will have. Even seasonal locations, like fairs or amusement parks, contain a large enough amount of energy that dirt can be harvested from them and worked with year-round.

Like with other locations, developing a relationship with the spirit of the land is important. Offerings still need to be given. Due to the nature of these locations and the amount of people typically there, there are often more difficulties when it comes to developing relationships with these spirits and gathering dirt.

For social spaces, it is especially important to be mindful of the hours of operation as well as when these locations are busiest. It may take a lot of observation before you are able to find a time and location that works best for you. The more time and effort you put into the work of gathering dirt, the more power the dirt will have for your magic. As always, obey trespassing laws.

Malls & Shopping Centers

Dirt from malls and shopping centers has a variety of magical functions. One of the major uses is that of money work. Lots of money is spent at malls and shopping centers.

INCREASE SALES PACKET CHARM

Here is a spell to attract sales and money to your own life or business.

MATERIALS
- Copy of a receipt or invoice from your business
- Small magnet (for attraction)
- 1 tablespoon (15 ml) mall dirt (for money, sales)
- 1 tablespoon (15 ml) cinquefoil (*Potentilla simplex*) (for fast cash)
- Small iron pyrite (for money, prosperity)
- 2 feet (61 cm) green ribbon

WORKING

1. Place the receipt or invoice face up. Set the magnet in the center of the paper, saying:

   To attract sales.

2. Sprinkle the mall dirt over the magnet and state:

   For sales.

3. Add the cinquefoil and state:

   For fast cash.

4. Place the iron pyrite on top of the dirt and cinquefoil. State:

   For prosperity and success.

5. Fold the receipt or invoice toward you, covering the materials as best you can.

6. Continue to fold the paper toward you until all paper is folded and a small packet has been created.

7. Wrap the ribbon around the packet five times, stating:

   Sales flowing freely. Customers leaving happily.

8. After the fifth pass, tie a knot with the ribbon to seal the energy in the packet.

9. Place the packet either under your register or next to your invoice station. As long as you keep the packet near your register or invoice station, you will have a steady increase in sales.

10. To keep the packet activated, play with it at least once a day, thinking about increased sales and new customers.

11. When you no longer need the packet, dispose of it in the trash near or around your business.

GAIN NEW FRIENDS POWDER

Shopping areas are full of socializing people and great places to meet new people and develop those contacts into friendships. This makes dirt harvested from malls and similar areas ideal for magic dealing with relationships.

The goal of this spell is to help you gain new friends and social contacts. This spell involves burning paper. For safety, perform the spell in a clear area outside and have a fire extinguisher or bowl of water nearby.

MATERIALS
- Fire extinguisher or bowl of water
- Pen
- Paper
- Firesafe bowl
- Lighter or matches
- 4 teaspoons (20 ml) mall dirt (for friends, socialization)
- 2 tablespoons (30 ml) crushed or ground passionflower (*Passiflora incarnata*) (for friendship, love between friends)

- 1 tablespoon (15 ml) ground yellow rose petals (*Rosa*) (for friendship)
- Spoon or wand
- Small storage container with lid
- Label sticker

WORKING

1. Clear your outdoor workspace of any flammable materials, and place the fire extinguisher or bowl of water nearby.

2. On the paper, write out your desire to make new friends and connections. Include the interests and hobbies that you would like to share with these friends.

3. Place the paper in the firesafe bowl and set it on fire.

4. As the paper burns, see yourself making new friends and additional connections. Feel yourself surrounded by friends and allies that support and care for you. Direct those emotions and images into the paper.

5. Once the paper has completely burned and the ash has cooled, add the mall dirt to the bowl. As you add the dirt, state:

    To open the roads to new connections and friendships.

6. Sprinkle the passionflower into the bowl and state:

    To bring friends that are new. Bring me friends who will be loyal and true.

7. Add the yellow rose petals, stating:

   For the love between friends.

8. Use the wand or spoon to mix the materials together thoroughly. As you stir, focus on feeling the love of friends all around you. See yourself meeting new friends and having new connections. Hold those images for as long as you can and direct that energy into the mixture, reciting the following chant seven to nine times:

   Make new friends today. Friends who by my side shall always stay.

9. Pour the mixture into the storage container and label the container "Gain New Friends Powder."

10. Before running out to do errands or go shopping, sprinkle a little bit of the powder mixture into your shoes. As you sprinkle the powder, state:

    With each step I do take, more new friends I do make.

11. Repeat step 10 until the powder is gone. Create more powder as needed.

ATTRACT DATES PACKET SPELL

This spell is for when you just want to date and get to know people. You aren't looking for a serious relationship, just someone to go out and do things with.

MATERIALS

- Small bowl
- 2 tablespoons (30 ml) mall dirt (for dating, relationships)
- 1 tablespoon (15 ml) sugar (for attraction)
- 1 tablespoon (15 ml) lavender (*Lavandula angustifolia*) (for happiness, love)
- 1 tablespoon (15 ml) cinnamon (*Cinnamomum verum*) (for love, lust, sexuality)
- Spoon or wand
- Pen
- Paper
- 6 to 8 inches (15–20 cm) red ribbon
- Scissors

WORKING

1. Begin by placing the mall dirt in the bowl. As you add the dirt, state:

   Dirt of the mall, place where many date, open the gate for the dates that await.

2. Add the sugar to the bowl and state:

   With sugar that is sweet, interesting people I will meet.

3. Sprinkle the lavender into the bowl. State:

   For happiness, peace, and love between us.

4. Add the cinnamon, stating:

   May there be a touch of lust and sexuality as well.

5. Use the spoon or wand to mix the materials together. As you stir, focus on the types of people you want to date and what sort of relationships you want to have. Direct that energy into the mixture. Once the mixture is thoroughly mixed, set it aside.

6. In the center of the paper, write out your desire to go on dates and have fun.

7. Cover the writing with the powder you just created.

8. Fold both ends of the paper toward the center. Rotate the paper 90 degrees and fold both sides toward the center again.

9. Wrap the ribbon around the bundle until you feel it is covered and it can be securely tied. Tie a knot in the ribbon.

10. Carry the packet with you any time you go out and about to run errands. It will attract the type of person you want to date. Keep carrying the packet with you until you have attracted the person or people you want to date.

11. To dispose of the packet, use scissors to cut the ribbon and toss the packet into the trash.

Beauty Salons

Hair and beauty salons are great places to harvest dirt for beauty and self-esteem work. The energy from beauty treatments seeps into the location and gathering dirt from a salon floor allows you to bring the feelings associated with a trip to the salon into your spellwork.

SELF-LOVE, SELF-ESTEEM BOOST CHARM

Use this spell to create a simple charm to carry with you when you need a boost in confidence and self-esteem.

MATERIALS
- Pink or yellow drawstring bag
- Hair or other personal effect of yours
- 3 tablespoons (45 ml) salon dirt (for self-care, self-esteem, self-love)
- 2 tablespoons (30 ml) sunflower seeds (*Helianthus annuus*) (for hope, light, love)
- Petals from 1 fresh pink rose (*Rosa*) (for self-love)
- Small rose quartz (for self-love)
- 1 tablespoon (15 ml) sugar (for looking at yourself favorably, sweetening disposition)

WORKING
1. Place your personal effect in the bag. As you add the personal effect, state:

   Effect that is mine, self-love deep inside shall now shine.

2. Add the dirt from the salon. As you sprinkle the dirt into the bag, state:

   Salon of beauty that makes me smile, help me hold this feeling for a while.

231

3. Add the sunflower seeds to the bag. As you add the seeds, state:

> *Sunflowers that grow sky high, help my spirit to smile and fly.*

4. Gently place the rose petals in the bag. As you add each petal, state:

> *Soft pink rose of self-love, my self-doubt away shove.*

5. Place the rose quartz in the bag. As you add it, state:

> *Rose quartz that is a stone, with your help self-love is known.*

6. Pull or tie the bag closed.

7. Mix the ingredients within the bag by holding the bag and playing with it. As you do so, chant:

> *Self-love within grow. Let this love show.*

8. Carry the bag with you daily as long as you feel the need for the boost. Any time you start to feel self-doubt or anything similar, play with the charm to center and refocus your energy.

9. When you no longer need the charm, dispose of the dirt and herbs as you see fit. Cleanse the crystal and bag to be used in other magical works.

To Feel Sexy Powder

A trip to a beauty salon is a great way to feel sexy, beautiful, and desired. Use this spell when you have not been feeling particularly sexy or beautiful.

MATERIALS
- Small bowl
- Spoon or wand
- 1 tablespoon (15 ml) salon dirt (to feel sexy)
- 1 tablespoon (15 ml) patchouli leaf (*Pogostemon cablin*) (for attraction, beauty, sexuality)
- Ground petals from 1 red rose (*Rosa*) (for beauty, love)
- 3 ground juniper berries (*Juniperus communis*) (for love and to protect feelings of love)
- 1 tablespoon (15 ml) ginseng (*Panax ginseng*) (for beauty, desire, lust, sexuality)
- 2 ounces (57 gram) baby powder
- Empty 3-ounce (85-gram) spice jar with shaker lid
- Pen and label sticker

WORKING
1. Add the dirt, herbal materials, and baby powder to the bowl. As you add each of the materials, state why it is being used.

2. Mix all of the materials together. As you stir, concentrate and focus on how you see yourself when you feel your sexiest. Hold on to that image for as long as possible. When you can no longer hold on to the image, release the energy,

directing it down your arms and hands and into the mixture through the spoon or wand.

3. Carefully pour the mixture into the old spice jar.

4. Label the jar "To Feel Sexy Powder," and store it in a dry, cool, and dark place. Kept out of the sun and away from moisture, the powder will last 12 to 14 months.

5. When you need the boost, carefully dust the powder under your armpits, across your chest, and in your shoes. As you sweat and go about your day, the energy within the powder will be activated and you will begin to feel sexier and more attractive.

LOOSE LIPS, HOT LIPS— A STOP GOSSIP CURSE

The town beauty salon is often a place of gossip. When you need to stop someone from spreading rumors about you, work with the dirt from their favorite beauty salon.

This spell will cause the individual who is spreading rumors to feel pain when they speak. Wear gloves while handling the jalapeño pepper (*Capsicum annuum*).

MATERIALS
- Gloves
- Knife
- Fresh jalapeño pepper (for baneful magic, cursing)

- Pen
- Slip of paper
- 1 pinch salon dirt (for gossip)
- Needle
- 1 foot (30.5 cm) black thread
- 5 pins

WORKING

1. While wearing the gloves, use the knife to cut open the jalapeño pepper. Remove the membrane and seeds from the pepper.

2. On one side of the paper, write the words "Stop Gossip." On the other side of the paper, write the name of the person who has been gossiping and spreading rumors. If their name is not known, write "Stop Gossip" once again.

3. Sprinkle the dirt from the salon over the slip of paper. As you sprinkle the dirt, state:

   Spreading gossip and lies is not right. Pain when you speak till you see the light.

4. Fold up the paper, leaving as much dirt in the paper as possible.

5. Set the folded piece of paper in the cut pepper.

6. Use the needle and thread to stitch the pepper closed. As you stitch, see your target's mouth being glued together, rendering them unable to spread lies or rumors.

7. Once the pepper has been stitched closed, stick the pins along the stitches.

8. Keep the stuffed pepper somewhere dark and dry. Leave it undisturbed until you feel your target has learned their lesson.

9. Once the lesson has been learned, you can toss the whole pepper into a trash can away from your home or place of work. If you wish to save the pins, simply remove them before discarding the pepper. You can cleanse the pins with salt and soap and water.

Spas & Massage Parlors

Spas are wonderful places to heal. They provide physical healing as well as relief from emotional tension. These locations also provide a great way for loved ones to reconnect and heal their relationships.

RELIEVE SORE MUSCLES HEALING POPPET

Sometimes we just overdo it a little bit. This spell is for times like those, when we go just a little over what we can physically do, and it will help heal and relieve pain from sore muscles.

MATERIALS
- Mixing bowl
- Spoon or wand
- 3 pinches massage parlor dirt (for healing, pain relief)
- 1 cup (250 ml) salt

- 1 cup (250 ml) water
- 2 cups (500 ml) flour
- 2 tablespoons (30 ml) ground arnica flowers (*Arnica montana*) (for healing, pain relief)
- 1 tablespoon (15 ml) lavender (*Lavandula angustifolia*) (for healing, pain relief)
- Baking sheet
- 2 tablespoons (30 ml) cayenne powder (*Capsicum annuum*) (for healing, pain relief)
- 2 tablespoons (30 ml) ground peppermint (*Mentha × piperita*) (for healing, pain relief)
- Small bowl

WORKING

1. In the bowl, mix half of the dirt with the salt, water, flour, arnica flowers, and lavender. Mix until you have a pliable dough.

2. Lay the dough out on the baking sheet, and shape it into a rough human shape. Once complete, state:

   Doll of dough, I name you: (target).

3. Mix the remaining dirt, cayenne pepper, and ground peppermint together in the second bowl. While you mix the materials, repeat the following chant five to seven times:

   Heal the pain of (name) today. Pain and suffering go away.

4. Apply the mixture to the dough body. If you are focusing on a specific area, apply the mixture to

that area. Otherwise, carefully apply the mixture to the entire figure.

5. Once the mixture has been applied, hold your hands over the dough doll and direct some healing energy into it. (I like to use blue and green healing light.) Hold on to the images as long as possible. When you can no longer hold on to the images and energy, release the energy into the doll. The doll will absorb the healing energy and send it to the person you named it for.

6. Let the dough doll dry. As it does, the healing energy will be sent to the person you are doing the healing for. Once the doll has dried, the healing is complete.

7. With the healing complete, you can dispose of the doll. If possible, dispose of it outside where it can biodegrade. Otherwise, dispose of it in the trash.

Bring Peace to Chaos Candle Spell

When we are under stress, our thought patterns often become chaotic and can be overwhelming. This spell will help calm down those thoughts and bring a sense of peace into your life.

MATERIALS
- Pen
- Paper

- 1 tablespoon (15 ml) dirt from the massage parlor (to bring peace)
- 1 tablespoon (15 ml) lavender (*Lavandula angustifolia*) (for peace, stress relief)
- 1 tablespoon (15 ml) chamomile (*Matricaria chamomilla*) (for peace, stress relief)
- 1 tablespoon (15 ml) peppermint (*Mentha* × *piperita*) (for peace, stress relief)
- Brain- or skull-shaped candle
- Candleholder
- Lighter or matches

WORKING

1. Draw a large circle on the paper. The circle's size depends on how many things you are stressed out about.

2. In the circle, write out a list of the things that are causing you stress.

3. Scatter the dirt over the circle. As you do so, state:

   Place of peace, bring stress relief.

4. Place the herbs in the shape of a peace sign on top of the stressors, beginning with the lavender. As you sprinkle the lavender, state:

   Peace of mind is easy to find.

5. Add the peppermint to continue making the peace sign. As you add the herb, state:

   Peppermint to slow down so a solution may be found.

6. Finish the peace sign by sprinkling the chamomile. State:

    Peace and calm for today keeps the harm of stress away.

7. Place the candleholder in the center of the peace sign and set the candle in it. Light the candle. As the candle burns, state:

    By the candle's gentle glow, peace and calm shall I know.

8. As the candle burns, feel your thoughts slow down and feel yourself becoming more relaxed and less stressed. Let the candle burn out. If you are unable to burn the candle in one sitting, burn the candle for 5 minutes a day until it has burned completely. Each time you light the candle, recite the statement from step 7.

9. When the candle has completely burned, dispose of the materials in the trash.

Casinos

Luck is an important aspect of our life that often gets ignored. Good luck can bring in new opportunities, manifest money, and have things go your way, while bad luck causes problems. If you need to perform luck magic, dirt from a casino works wonderfully.

INCREASE LUCK SPRAY

This spell is for when you are playing friendly games at home and you want to stack the odds in your favor.

Be aware that this spell takes time, as you are making an infused anointing oil, which can be used in any other luck work.

MATERIALS
- 12-ounce (340-gram) mason jar with lid
- Pinch of casino dirt (for gambling luck)
- 1 tablespoon (15 ml) nutmeg (*Myristica fragrans*) (for good luck)
- Dried and ground peel from 1 orange (*Citrus × sinensis*) (for good luck)
- 5 dried raspberries (*Rubus idaeus* var. *strigosus*) (for good luck and to attract luck)
- Iron pyrite (for luck)
- 1 cup (250 ml) 70 to 90 proof vodka, rum, or everclear
- Cheesecloth
- Spray bottle
- Pen and label sticker

WORKING
1. Start by adding the dirt to the jar. As you add the dirt, state:

   Casino dirt for luck.

2. Pour the ground nutmeg and orange peels into the jar. As you add these materials, state:

   Sweet and spice brings luck that is nice.

3. Seal the jar and shake it to mix the materials thoroughly. While shaking the jar, repeat the following chant five times:

   With money and cash at stake, good luck to win is my fate.

4. Open the jar and add the raspberries one at a time. As you add each berry, state:

   Berry that is sour brings great luck in this hour.

5. Repeat step 3.

6. Open the jar and add the iron pyrite.

7. Pour the alcohol into the jar. You want to make sure the jar is filled almost to the top.

8. Seal the jar and shake it vigorously. While you shake the jar, repeat the same chant as before seven to nine times.

9. Set the jar in a location that is dry, cool, and dark.

10. Repeat step 8 twice a day for the next 5 weeks.

11. Set the cheesecloth across the opening of the spray bottle.

12. Carefully unseal the jar and slowly begin to pour the liquid into the spray bottle. You may need to pause every so often to squeeze the liquid from the remnants in the cheesecloth.

13. Once the bottle is full, remove the cheesecloth. Set the iron pyrite aside to cleanse. The cheese-cloth, including all materials in it, can be tossed in the trash.

14. Seal the spray bottle and label it "Good Luck Spray." Store it out of direct sunlight. The bottle will stay charged and effective for 6 to 9 months.

15. Before playing games, spritz yourself with the spray. If you have any other good luck charms, spraying them will give them a boost as well. When hosting a game night, you can spray the room once in the center to bring luck to every-one. To enhance your luck, anoint the cards or other game tools before the others arrive and you begin to play.

SIMPLE LUCK CHARM

This is a simple charm that can be carried with you daily to bring a little good luck into your everyday life.

MATERIALS
- Small glass halfway full of water
- 1 teaspoon (5 ml) sugar (for attraction, speed and to sweeten luck)
- 1 teaspoon (5 ml) nutmeg (*Myristica fragrans*) (for good luck)
- ½ teaspoon (2.5 ml) honey or maple (*Acer*) syrup (for attraction and to sweeten luck, stick to you)
- Paintbrush

- 3 pinches casino dirt (for good luck)
- 1 flat gold stone that fits in the palm of your hand (for good luck)

WORKING

1. Add the sugar, cinnamon, and honey or maple syrup to the water. Use the paintbrush to stir the mixture. As you stir the mixture, state:

   Good luck come to me. My lucky day this shall be.

2. Sprinkle the casino dirt into the water. Use the paintbrush to stir the mixture. As you stir, repeat the following chant five to seven times:

   Good luck today. Luck comes my way.

3. Use the mixture to paint the symbol of the sun on one side of the palm stone. While you paint the symbol, state:

   Luck coming to me brings prosperity.

4. Let the symbol dry. Once it has, flip the stone over. On this side, paint the symbol for the planet Jupiter. Repeat the same statement as before.

5. Let the charm dry. Once it has, carry the charm with you when you need an extra boost of luck. Dispose of the water down the drain. The charm

will last for 1 month. Repeat the working as needed.

Pubs, Bars & Nightclubs

For as long as they have been around, pubs, bars, and nightclubs have been places of social gathering. These spots are great places for relaxing and having some fun with friends or dates. All this socializing means the dirt from these locations may be used to help you obtain any type of relationship you want to have.

DESIRE DATES POWDER

This spell is for when you are trying to attract people to date. Note that this spell is not for finding a steady and committed relationship; it is for casual dating to have fun and enjoy each other's company.

MATERIALS
- Small bowl
- 3 tablespoons (45 ml) dirt from your local bar, nightclub, or pub (for dating relationships)
- Mortar and pestle
- 2 tablespoons (30 ml) cardamom (*Elettaria cardamomum*) (for lust)
- 1 tablespoon (15 ml) coriander seeds (*Coriandrum sativum*) (for love spells)
- ½ tablespoon (7.5 ml) catnip (*Nepeta cataria*) (for friendship, happiness, relationships)
- ¼ cup (60 ml) baby powder

- Spoon or wand
- Juniper essential oil (*Juniperus communis*) (for love)
- Storage container
- Pen and label sticker

WORKING

1. Place the dirt in the bowl. As you add the dirt, state:

   Dirt from a club or bar, bring me dates from near and far.

2. Use the mortar and pestle to grind the cardamom into a fine powder. Direct the physical energy you are using to grind the herb into it, focusing on your desire for dates and good times. Repeat the following chant until the cardamom is as finely ground as possible:

   Bring lust to me, attracting dates freely.

   Transfer the ground cardamom into the bowl with the dirt.

3. Place the coriander in the mortar and use the pestle to grind it into a fine powder. While you grind the coriander, direct the physical energy you are using to grind the herb into it, focusing on your desire for dates and good times. Repeat the following chant until it is as finely ground as possible:

   Companionship to go out and date is my desired fate.

   Transfer the ground coriander into the bowl with the dirt and cardamom.

4. Sprinkle the catnip into the bowl and use the spoon or wand to mix the materials together. As you stir, repeat the following chant five to seven times:

   Happiness comes with new dates for me.

5. Add the baby powder to the mixture while you stir. As you add the powder and mix, repeat the following chant five to seven times:

   Dating casually, make me happy.

6. Add 5 to 7 drops of the juniper essential oil to the powder. With each drop of oil, state:

   Love and lust in dating are a must.

7. Stir in the oil.

8. Once the materials are well mixed, hold your hands over the powder and focus on shaping all of the energy you have raised into a single cohesive force. Direct that force into the powder, charging it with energy for fun, dating, and friendship. When you can no longer hold on to the energy, release it into the powder.

9. Transfer the powder into the storage container. Label the container "Desire Dates Powder." Store the powder away from light and moisture.

10. Before you go out for the evening, sprinkle a little of this powder over the outside of your underwear, in your armpits, and in your shoes. Repeat this process every time you go out looking for

dates or on a date. Create a new batch of powder after 3 months.

ATTRACT A ROMANTIC RELATIONSHIP SPELL

This spell is for when you are ready to go from dating to a serious and steady relationship. Use the working to attract the right romantic partner to your life. Remember to focus on the goal itself and not a specific individual.

MATERIALS
- Large plate
- 2 human dolls
- Candleholder
- Large red candle
- Pin, needle, or knife
- ¼ cup (60 ml) beet juice (*Beta vulgaris*) (for love)
- Paintbrush
- 3 pinches dirt from your local bar, nightclub, or pub (for dating, relationships)
- 1 teaspoon (5 ml) sugar (for attraction)
- Petals from 3 red roses (*Rosa*) (for love, romance)
- 1 tablespoon (15 ml) catnip (*Nepeta cataria*) (for love, relationships)
- 1 teaspoon (5 ml) cinnamon (*Cinnamomum verum*) (for love, lust)
- 1 tablespoon (15 ml) yellow dock (*Rumex crispus*) (for love)
- Lighter or matches

WORKING

1. In the center of the plate, place the two figures together. If possible, have them holding hands or embracing in some way. As you position the two figures, state:

   One figure is to be me, the other a partner who loves me truly.

2. If the candleholders cannot safely fit on the plate with the figures, place the candleholders in front of the plate, between the figures. If the candleholders can safely fit on the plate between the two figures, then place the candleholders on the plate.

3. Use the pin, needle, or knife to carve two hearts intertwined on both sides of the candle. As you carve the hearts, chant:

   Love that is true, love that is new.

4. Set the candle into the holder.

5. Dip the paintbrush into the beet juice and paint a heart around the candle and the two figures. As you paint, repeat the chant from step 3 three times.

6. Sprinkle the dirt along the lines of the heart. As you sprinkle the dirt, state:

   Dirt from a club I visit frequently, bring a love that's true to me.

7. Repeat the statement until the heart has been completely traced with dirt.

8. Sprinkle the sugar along the heart, stating:

   *With sugar that is sweet, a love that's true
   I will surely meet.*

9. Repeat the statement until the heart has been traced with sugar.

10. Carefully place the rose petals along the lines of the heart. As you place the petals, state:

    Love for me on this day. True love will find its way.

11. Repeat the statement until the heart has been traced three times with rose petals.

12. Sprinkle the catnip along the heart. As you sprinkle the catnip, state:

    Happiness, from a deep love, seems like a gift from heaven above.

13. Repeat the statement until the heart has been traced with the catnip.

14. Sprinkle the cinnamon powder in a circle around the two figures. State:

    Lust is that which sparks the fire and makes the passion rise higher.

15. Add the yellow dock along the heart. State:

    Yellow dock for love to draw from people who live near and far.

16. Light the candle. As you do so, state:

    By this candle's soft glowing light, true love comes my way this night.

17. Let the candle burn out completely. If you are unable to burn the entire candle in one sitting, then burn the candle for 5 to 10 minutes a day. Once the candle has been burned completely, dispose of the herbs in the trash. Wash the plate. The figures can be cleansed to be used in future magical work, washed and kept for your enjoyment, or they can be given to a child to play with.

ROAD TO RECOVERY CANDLE SPELL

Alcoholism is a terrible disease that impacts many people across the world. As witches and magical workers, we often want to provide healing to those we care about if they need it. One of the tools that can be added to the magical arsenal to help heal alcoholism is dirt harvested from pubs, bars, and liquor stores.

This spell uses such dirt to try and get your loved one to listen to you and stop their drinking before it's too late. Remember that recovering from addiction takes time and effort. This spell just helps them take those first few steps. The rest is up to them.

Know that this spell is dangerous and should only be performed with the full consent of the target and their loved ones. Before performing this spell, it is also important to contact both a primary care provider and a mental health specialist to go over any and all health risks associated with the removal of alcohol from the body. Addictions can harm the body in many unknown and unseen ways. Make sure you understand all the health risks before starting this process. The last thing you want is for the healing work to cause more harm than good.

The recipe for healing anointing oil can be found in part 3. You will want enough to cover the candle from the base to the wick.

MATERIALS
- Blue pen
- Image of a maze
- Candleholder
- Blue taper candle
- Pin, needle, or knife
- 7 to 9 drops healing anointing oil
- Small bowl
- Spoon or wand
- 3 pinches dirt from a liquor store, pub, or bar (to heal alcoholism)
- 3 tablespoons (45 ml) sugar (for sweetening)
- 1 tablespoon (15 ml) rosemary (*Salvia osmarinus*) (for family and friends, healing, mental powers, opening the mind)
- ½ tablespoon (7.5 ml) lavender (*Lavandula angustifolia*) (for healing, mental health healing, the mind)
- 1 tablespoon (15 ml) feverfew (*Tanacetum parthenium*) (for protection from illness, including alcoholism)

- ½ tablespoon (7.5 ml) plantain (*Plantago major*) (for healing, protection against self and previous behaviors, strength)
- Lighter or matches

WORKING

1. Across the top of the maze, write the words "Road to Recovery." In the center, where the goal is, write the word "Recovery."

2. Set the candleholder in front of the maze.

3. Use the pin, needle, or knife to carve the name of the person who needs the healing into the candle.

4. Anoint the candle with the healing oil. As you anoint the candle, state:

   Oil that helps one to heal, the road to recovery I ask you to reveal.

5. Place the candle into the holder.

6. Add the dirt, sugar, and herbs to the small bowl, and use the spoon or wand to mix the materials together, repeating the following chant until everything is thoroughly mixed, about seven to nine times:

   Healing herbs, I call upon thee. From addiction and illness (name) is now free.

7. Once the materials have been thoroughly mixed together, use the pen to solve the maze.

8. Sprinkle the herbal mixture over the path to the center or goal. As you sprinkle the mixture, repeat the statement:

   Healing for (name) until the path has been completed.

9. Light the candle. As you light the candle, state:

   By this candle's soothing, healing light, recovery and healing for (name) is now in sight.

10. Let the candle burn for 5 minutes, then extinguish the candle.

11. Move the candleholder down the healing path. Keep the candle there for a day.

12. For the next several days, until the candle has been fully burned, repeat steps 9 through 11 until the candle has reached the center goal. If the candle has burned completely when you reach the goal, you can dispose of the materials as you see fit and go about your life knowing the healing energy has been sent to your target. If the candle has not fully burned, continue to light the candle for 5 minutes a day until it has completely burned. At that point, you can dispose of the materials.

CROSSROADS

When it comes to magical work, crossroads are one of the most popular locations to talk about. Crossroads have long been seen as places full of spirits and mysteries. These are locations where two roads cross and form an intersection, creating a liminal space. Liminal spaces are those that border two different locations. When it comes to spiritual work, liminal spaces are both in the physical world and within the spiritual realms.

The power of these locations comes from the fact that they are stationed between worlds, and that liminal energy can be used to power any spell and send the magic out in all directions.

One of the more traditional ways to work with crossroads is to bury the remains of workings at them. By doing this you are sending that energy into the spiritual realms and out in the four directions. Burial of spellwork at a crossroads ensures that the energy is dispersed across the universe, providing an effective route for your desire to manifest. This method should only be used if the materials you are burying are biodegradable.

Another way to work with crossroads dirt is to use it to power your spells. Crossroads dirt, even used away from its source, will send the magical work you do in the four cardinal directions to manifest your goal quickly.

In this chapter, I will share spells for many purposes, ranging from love to luck. But first, with crossroads being liminal spaces, it is important to do some prep before you gather the dirt. Crossroads are home to a variety of spiritual forces. Some of those forces may have ill intent toward you. The preparatory work prevents them from being able to cause mischief in your life.

Preparatory Work

If you gather dirt from crossroads without doing any preparation, there is no saying how the spirits could act toward you and how the chaos could unfold. There are many different spirits that live at crossroads. Some of those spirits are trickster spirits, and others are simply demons or various evil spirits. Often these spirits will offer you great power or the ability to have your heart's desire in an instant. When these items are offered, there is typically a catch, and the spirits will try to trick you out of the reward that they promised you.

Protection charms will keep those negative spirits away from you by either having you see through the spirits' trickery or by completely repelling them from your presence. The best protection charms are those that both repel evil and negativity and harm or destroy it, but as long as your protection charm does one of those two things, you will be fine.

BIRCH COIN REPEL & PROTECT TALISMAN

Birch trees (*Betula pendula*) are known to repel evil. This working makes a simple charm that you can carry in your pocket or wallet. It will protect you while you gather crossroads dirt.

The birch coin can be found at craft stores.

MATERIALS
- Small birch coin (for protection against evil)
- Silver paint
- Paintbrush

WORKING
1. On one side of the coin, paint a protective symbol. Use one of these symbols or create your own.

Celtic Knot

Hecate's Wheel

Helm of Awe

Thor's Hammer

Hamsa

2. While you paint the symbol, chant:

   ***Coin made of birch, repel baneful spirits
   from my path this day.***

3. Set the coin to dry.

4. Once the paint is dry, flip the coin over and paint
   another protective symbol. It can be the same

symbol or a different symbol. While painting, chant:

> *Coin made of birch, repel all evil on this day.*
> *Away from me all baneful forces shall stay.*

5. Let the coin dry.

6. Once the paint on the coin is dry, carry it with you when you need its protection.

Money, Employment & Luck Spells

Money magic works. Whenever I need a boost to my financial situation, I take the time and work money spells. From spells to get a job and increase sales to workings that protect cash flow, money magic is an effective tool to help you live your best life. Using crossroads dirt ensures that no matter which way the winds of change blow, you are always covered.

The fast-money powder can be found in part 3.

ATTRACT EMPLOYMENT PACKET SPELL

This spell is to help you land a job. In order for this spell to work, you still need to fill out applications, send in your resume, go to interviews, and so on. The goal of the working is to get prospective employers attracted to and interested in employing you.

MATERIALS

- Pen
- Paper
- 2 tablespoons (30 ml) crossroads dirt (for power and to send spell energy to the four cardinal directions)
- 2 tablespoons (30 ml) sugar (for attraction)
- Sprig fresh rosemary (*Salvia rosmarinus*) (to open the mind)
- 1 teaspoon (5 ml) cinnamon (*Cinnamomum verum*) (for money, prosperity, wealth)
- 2 feet (61 cm) green or gold ribbon

WORKING

1. On the paper, write out all the details you know about the type of work you are looking for. Include the field, pay, location, work culture, and so on.

2. Rotate the paper 90 degrees toward you.

3. Across the list of job specifications, write the words "Hire (your first and last name)" five times or until the list is covered.

4. Sprinkle the dirt, sugar, and herbs over the words one at a time. As you sprinkle each material, state:

   A job for me. Employed I shall be.

5. Fold the paper in half toward you. Rotate the paper 90 degrees toward you. Fold the paper in half toward you and rotate the paper 90 degrees toward you again. Repeat three times.

6. Wrap the ribbon around the packet. While you wrap, chant:

   A job for me. Employed I shall be.

7. Continue to wrap and chant until the packet is fully covered.

8. Tie a knot in the ribbon near the top to seal the packet. Carry the packet with you in your pocket or wallet. Before each application or interview, play with the packet, filling yourself with confidence. See yourself holding the desired position.

9. Once you are employed, toss the packet away in a trash can near your new place of work.

ABUNDANCE & PROSPERITY CRYSTAL GRID

Unfortunately, money is something we need to survive in this world, and this spell will help bring abundance into your life.

For this spell, you want to have a small table, shelf, or corner where you can set up and leave the crystal grid. If keeping the grid up full-time is not possible, set the grid up for at least an hour a day.

MATERIALS
- 5-to-10-inch (13-to-25.5-cm) tall quartz tower
- 5 citrine tumbles (for abundance, money, prosperity)
- 5 aventurine tumbles (for abundance, money, prosperity)

- 5 goldstone tumbles (for abundance, money, prosperity)
- 5 iron pyrite tumbles (for abundance, money, prosperity)
- 100 pennies
- 2 tablespoons (30 ml) crossroads dirt (for power)

WORKING

1. Set the quartz tower in the center of your chosen work area.

2. Use the citrine, aventurine, goldstone, and iron pyrite to create a circle around the quartz tower, alternating crystals.

3. Place the pennies in four lines going from the circle to the crystal tower. There should be one line of pennies in each cardinal direction.

4. Sprinkle the crossroads dirt over the crystals and pennies. As you sprinkle the dirt, state:

   Spirit of the crossroads, I ask of thee, send abundance, wealth, and prosperity here to me.

5. As long as you leave the crystals out in this formation, extra prosperity, abundance, and wealth will come to you.

LUCK BOOST CHARM BAG

Carry this charm with you when you need a boost of luck. Job interviews and playing games of chance are excellent times to have it with you. That being said, there are no guarantees, so spend and play at casinos responsibly.

MATERIALS
- Gold or yellow drawstring bag
- Personal effect
- 2 pinches crossroads dirt (for luck, power)
- Iron pyrite (for good luck)
- 5 dried bilberries (*Vaccinium myrtillus*) (for luck)
- 3 whole nutmeg kernels (*Myristica fragrans*) (for luck)
- 3 thyme sprigs (*Thymus vulgaris*) (for good luck)

WORKING
1. Add the personal effect to the bag. As you add it, state:

    May today be my lucky day. May everything go my way.

2. Add the dirt to the bag. As you add the dirt, state:

    Crossroads dirt, bring luck from near and far.

3. Place the iron pyrite in the bag, stating:

    Fool's gold, iron pyrite, I call upon your luck with this rite.

4. Add the bilberries to the bag. As you add each berry, state:

    Luck for me. Good luck to be.

5. Place the nutmeg kernels in the bag. As you add each one, state:

    Nutmeg that's sweet, with you, good luck shall I meet.

6. Add the thyme to the bag. State:

   By the power of this thyme, good luck brings a good time.

7. Pull the drawstring bag closed. Hold the bag between your hands and play with it for a few minutes, mixing the ingredients. While you manipulate the bag, feel good luck flowing to you. Know that luck is on your side.

8. Carry the charm with you while at the casino or a job interview. If you feel nervous, hold the charm and relax. Have fun and enjoy yourself. When you no longer wish to have the luck charm, you can dispose of the dirt and herbs. Cleanse the bag and stone, as they can be used in other magical work.

Psychic, Spiritual & Divination Work

One of the great things about crossroads dirt is its connection to the spiritual worlds and psychic abilities. The following spells use dirt from crossroads to aid in psychic and spiritual work. From divination to trance work and the use of general psychic senses, these spells can boost your personal practices.

CROSSROADS SKELETON KEY TALISMAN

Use this spell to create a charm to empower your trance and spirit world workings. It will help open the doors to the spiritual realms.

MATERIALS

- Small bowl
- Skeleton key (to open doors)
- 6 tablespoons (90 ml) crossroads dirt (to open doors and for spiritual realms)
- 3 tablespoons (45 ml) damiana leaf (*Turnera diffusa*) (for spiritual development, trance work)
- 2 small sticks

WORKING

1. Set the key in the bowl and cover it with the crossroads dirt and damiana leaf.

2. Hold your hands over the bowl and state:

   Key that belongs to no door, a key to the spirit world shall you be forever more.

3. Place the two small sticks across the dirt and damiana leaf.

4. Leave the key covered in the dirt and herbs for 24 hours. After 24 hours, the key is fully charged and ready for use. Keep it for future trance workings.

5. Dispose of the herbs and dirt. If possible, return the sticks to nature. When that is not possible, dispose of the sticks with the herbs and dirt.

6. To keep the key charged, repeat the spell every 4 to 6 weeks.

CROSSROADS DIRT DIVINATION WORKING

This divination working is a combination of reading tea leaves (tasseography) or smoke scrying (libanomancy) and stone reading (lithomancy) or bone and curio readings (osteomancy).

The recipe for meditation incense can be found in part 3. If you do not have a wand or stick, a stone pendulum with a point will also work.

MATERIALS
- Pen
- Paper
- Self-lighting charcoal disc
- Tongs
- Long-stemmed lighter
- Censer
- 1 tablespoon (15 ml) meditation incense
- Small mixing bowl
- 1 teaspoon (5 ml) thyme (*Thymus vulgaris*) (for divination, psychic powers, psychic senses)
- ½ teaspoon (2.5 ml) lavender (*Lavandula angustifolia*) (for mental focus, mental clarity, psychic powers, psychic senses)
- ½ teaspoon (2.5 ml) mugwort (*Artemisia vulgaris*) (for divination, psychic powers, psychic senses)
- 4 tablespoons (60 grams) crossroads dirt (for divination, psychic abilities and gifts, spiritual realms)

- Packet carrot seeds (*Daucus carota*) (for divination, psychic powers, psychic senses)
- 2 tablespoons (30 ml) poppy seeds (*Papaver somniferum*) (for altered states of consciousness)
- 3 crushed and ground star anise seeds (*Illicium verum*) (for awakening psychic powers, divination, psychic abilities, psychic powers)
- Spoon or wand
- Empty 3-ounce (85-gram) spice jar with shaker lid
- Label sticker
- Medium purple votive candle
- Votive candleholder
- Small plate
- Wand or long pointed stick
- Notebook
- Miniature broom

WORKING

1. On the paper, write out three different affirmations connected to your psychic senses and abilities. You may want to use something along the lines of: "My psychic senses grow stronger every day" or "My psychic senses are clear and accurate." Those are just two examples that I have used in my own practice. Take time and think about three goals you have for your powers of psychic sight. Try to write your affirmations around those goals.

2. Hold the charcoal disc with the tongs and use the long-stemmed lighter to light it. Once there are sparks flying across the charcoal disc, carefully

place it in the censer. Let the disc spark. Sprinkle the meditation incense over the charcoal, and let the incense smolder, creating smoke.

3. In the mixing bowl, combine all of the herbal materials. As you add each ingredient, state why you are working with it and what your goals are.

4. Mix the materials together. As you do so, recite each affirmation set five times. Then repeat each affirmation set three times more. Direct all of the energy generated down your arm and into the mixture.

5. Set the candle in its holder. Light it.

6. Pour the herbal mixture over the plate. Cover the plate with as much powder as possible.

7. Take a few breaths to ground and center yourself. After two to three breaths, close your eyes and hold the stick or wand in your hands. Move the tip of the stick or wand around the plate, drawing random lines in the herbs. While you draw, recite one of your previous affirmations ten times.

8. Once you have finished reciting your affirmation, set your drawing utensil aside. Open your eyes and take several moments to gently and carefully gaze into the lines in the dirt. Take note of any signs, symbols, or images you see.

9. When you can no longer hold your gaze, extinguish the candle and incense. In the notebook,

record what you saw and write out what you think the symbols and images mean together.

10. Once the charcoal ash has cooled, dispose of it in the trash. Carefully pour the herbal mixture into the spice jar. Label the mixture "Crossroads Dirt Divination Powder." Use the broom to sweep up any remaining powder. Add it to the jar.

11. Repeat this scrying exercise once a week to keep your psychic senses strong. The more often you do this exercise, the easier it will be to perform and the more you will see. You may continue to use the same candle until it burns out. Replace the candle and create more powder as needed. One batch will last about 2 to 3 months.

ENHANCE PSYCHIC GIFTS POWDER WORKING

Use this spell once a month to strengthen your psychic gifts and abilities. This powder not only helps enhance your gifts and abilities but will also charge a divination tool, deepening your relationship with it.

You can find the recipe for meditation incense in part 3.

MATERIALS
- Small bowl
- Spoon or wand
- 2 tablespoons (30 ml) crossroads dirt (for divination, psychic abilities and gifts, spiritual realms)

- ½ tablespoon (7.5 ml) wormwood (*Artemisia absinthium*) (for divination, psychic abilities, psychic gifts, spiritual work)
- ½ tablespoon (7.5 ml) damiana leaf (*Turnera diffusa*) (for divination, psychic abilities, psychic gifts, spiritual work)
- 1 tablespoon (15 ml) vervain (*Verbena hastata*) (for divination, meditation, psychic abilities, psychic gifts, spiritual work)
- Empty 3-ounce (85-gram) spice jar with shaker lid
- Pen and label sticker
- Censer
- Charcoal disc
- Long-stemmed lighter
- Tongs
- Purple pillar candle
- Pin, needle, or knife
- Pillar candleholder
- Small plate
- Favorite divination tool
- 1 tablespoon (15 ml) meditation incense

WORKING

1. Place the dirt and each of the herbs in the mixing bowl one at a time, stirring after each ingredient is added. As you add each material, state:

   To enhance and strengthen my divination work.

2. Continue to stir the mixture. As you do so, recite the following chant five to seven times or until the blend is thoroughly mixed:

May my readings be true and provide wisdom that is new.

3. Carefully transfer the mixture into the spice jar. Label the container "Enhance Divination Crossroads Powder."

4. Set the plate in the center of your workspace. Place the censer behind the plate.

5. Use the tongs to hold the charcoal, and light the charcoal with the long-stemmed lighter. Once the charcoal is sparking, carefully place the disc in the censer. Sprinkle the incense on the charcoal. Let it smolder.

6. Use the pin, needle, or knife to carve the psychic eye symbol into opposite sides of the candle.

Psychic Eye

7. Place the candleholder on the plate. Set the candle in the holder.

8. Shake some of the powder into your hands and rub it into the candle where you carved the psychic eyes.

9. Use your hands to sweep any powder that landed on the plate into a circle around the

candleholder. If there isn't enough powder, simply sprinkle more around the candleholder until there is a small circle around it.

10. Light the candle. State:

> *By this candle's light, I gain accurate psychic insight.*

11. Safely pass your divination tool over the candle flame five times, repeating the previous statement with each pass.

12. Pass the divination tool through the incense smoke. As you do so, recite the following chant three to five times:

> *Incense smoke, on this night, grant true wisdom and insight.*

13. Hold the divination tool in your dominant hand. With your other hand, sprinkle a little powder over the tool. As you do so, state:

> *Powder to enhance divination, on this night, guide my intuition to provide accurate and wise insight.*

14. Set the divination tool safely in front of the candle.

15. Close your eyes and meditate. Reflect on your divination skills and your intuition. Know that those skills are going to get stronger and that your readings will become more accurate. Feel your skills grow.

16. If you wish to perform a reading, do so now. Otherwise, extinguish the candles and incense. Dispose of the used powder in the trash. Place the container of powder in storage with the censer, charcoal, and incense.

17. Repeat the spell once a month to strengthen your connection to your chosen divination tool. Replace the candle and make more powder as needed.

Crossroads Healing

Healing magic was the first area of magic I ever explored as a witch, and to this day, even after all my many years practicing, healing magic is still one of my strong suits. I like to combine modern techniques, such as aromatherapy and modern Reiki, with traditional spellwork.

One of the older magical tools in my healing magic kit is that of crossroads dirt. Crossroads dirt is a wonderful tool in healing magic, as it sends the healing energy out into the universe in the four cardinal directions.

DISTANCE CROSSROADS HEALING POPPET

This spell is an excellent choice when it comes to distance healing.

This spell involves sewing a poppet together. If stitching is not possible, that's okay. There are

fabric glues that will work just as well. The recipe
for healing anointing oil can be found in part 3.

MATERIALS

- 2 2-by-3-inch (5-by-8-cm) pieces of blue fabric
- Pen
- Scissors
- Needle
- 2 feet (61 cm) dark blue thread
- 5 tablespoons (75 ml) crossroads dirt (for healing power)
- 1 tablespoon (15 ml) lavender (*Lavandula angustifolia*) (for healing)
- 1 tablespoon (15 ml) marigold (*Calendula officinalis*) (for healing)
- 1 tablespoon (15 ml) lemon zest (*Citrus × limon*) (for cleansing)
- 1 tablespoon (15 ml) lemon balm (*Melissa officinalis*) (for healing)
- Small bowl
- Spoon
- Blue taper candle
- 5 to 7 drops healing anointing oil
- Candleholder
- Lighter or matches

WORKING

1. Place one piece of fabric on top of the other,
   and use the pen to draw a rough human shape.
   Use as much of the fabric as you can. You
   want a decent-sized form. Once the drawing is

complete, cut along the lines and through both layers of fabric.

2. Using the needle and blue thread, begin to stitch up the sides of the poppet, starting near the head. Leave the head open so you can fill the poppet.

3. Add the dirt and herbal materials to the bowl one at a time. As you add each item, state why it is being used. Use the spoon to mix the materials together. As you stir, recite the following statement five times:

   Crossroads near and far, send healing to (name of the person who needs healing). By the power of the compass round, where the four directions abound, can healing for (name) be found.

4. Use the spoon to fill the poppet with the mix.

5. Once the poppet has been filled, stitch the head closed.

6. Take the poppet in your hands and spread the materials throughout it. Once the materials have been thoroughly mixed and spread, set the poppet down.

7. Anoint the candle from the bottom to the top with the healing oil, then place the candle in its holder.

8. Hold the poppet before you and exhale into it. State:
   Poppet, I name you (name of person who needs healing).

9. Set the poppet in front of the candle.

10. Light the candle. As the candle burns bright, state:

   > **As this candle burns bright, healing energy sent to (name) through its light.**

11. Let the candle burn for 10 minutes. Extinguish the candle.

12. Every day until the candle has burned out, anoint both the candle and the poppet with healing oil and let the candle burn for 10 minutes before extinguishing. Once the candle has burned out, dispose of the poppet and other materials in a trash can near your home.

CROSSROADS FERTILITY SPELL

This spell calls upon the power of the four cardinal directions and Western elements to aid your fertility.

Only perform this spell if you and your partner are on the same page about having children and both agree to raise any children in as healthy and happy an environment as possible.

MATERIALS
- Small bowl
- 5 crushed acorns (*Quercus alba*) (for fertility, strength)
- 5 to 7 crushed banana chips (*Musa acuminata, Musa balbisiana*) (for fertility)
- 5 tablespoons (75 ml) crossroads dirt (for fertility, healing health, power)

- 1 tablespoon (15 ml) alfalfa (*Medicago sativa*) (for fertility)
- Dried avocado pit (*Persea americana*) (for fertility)
- Small knife
- Small plate

WORKING

1. In the bowl, combine the crushed acorns and banana chips, crossroads dirt, and alfalfa.

2. Use your hands to mix the ingredients together. As you do so, focus on having a safe and healthy pregnancy. See yourself with a happy and healthy baby. Direct all of that energy down your arms, through your hands, and into the mixture.

3. Carefully carve the rune Othala into one side of the avocado pit. Carve the rune Berkana into the other side.

4. Place the carved avocado pit on the plate.

5. Sprinkle the dirt and herbal mixture around the avocado pit, creating a circle. As you sprinkle the powder, focus on the fertility of you and your partner. See you both having the family that you want to have.

6. Once the circle is complete, hold your hands over the plate and state:

    By the powers of the runes Berkana, the power of the birch tree, and Othala, the

power of our ancestors, may we be blessed
with fertility and a family of our own.

7. Set the plate under your bed. When you sleep on the bed, the fertility charm will be active.

8. Dispose of the charm once you have confirmed a child has been conceived.

DEPRESSION RELIEF PACKET

Depression can be a disabling illness, and many of the early spells I performed in my healing work were done to help me manage my depression.

This spell will not heal your depression, but it will make it easier to have good days and enjoy yourself.

Only perform this spell when you or your target has taken the appropriate mundane actions, such as seeing a doctor or therapist. Depression can get severe quickly. For best results, perform this spell with the approval of a therapist or another medical professional.

MATERIALS
- Small yellow drawstring bag
- Hair or personal effect of the individual who needs healing
- 1 tablespoon (15 ml) crossroads dirt (for healing)
- 1 tablespoon (15 ml) sunflower seeds (*Helianthus annuus*) (for depression relief, hope)
- 1 tablespoon (15 ml) Saint-John's-wort (*Hypericum perforatum*) (for happiness, hope, depression relief)

- ½ tablespoon (7.5 ml) lavender (*Lavandula angustifolia*) (for depression relief, happiness, healing, hope)
- ½ tablespoon (7.5 ml) chamomile (*Matricaria recutita*) (for depression relief, happiness, healing, hope)
- 3 small rose quartz tumbles (for depression relief, happiness, healing, hope)
- 2 small amethyst tumbles (for depression relief, happiness, healing, hope)

WORKING

1. Begin by placing the personal effect in the drawstring bag. As you place the effect, state:

   Healing for (name) on this day. Blessings and good things come their way.

2. Place the remaining materials in the bag one at a time, stating:

   Healing for (name) today. Darkness of depression go away. Blessings and happiness may stay.

3. Once all of the materials have been added to the bag, pull it closed.

4. Play with the bag to mix the materials together. As you do so, direct feelings of healing, happiness, and depression relief into the bag. Maintain those feelings as long as you can. When you can no longer hold on to those feelings and images, release them into the bag.

5. Give the charm bag to the individual who needs the healing. Tell them to play with it when their depression is at its worst for the greatest healing effect. The charm bag will last for as long as the person uses it.

Love, Lust & Relationship Spells

Love can be hard to find. When you work love spells for yourself using crossroads dirt, you open up doors and pathways for love to find you from places you might have not thought about previously.

FULL OF LOVE CANDLE SPELL

This spell will fill your life with love of all sorts.

MATERIALS
- Red pillar candle
- Pin, needle, or knife
- Candleholder
- Small plate
- Petals from 1 red rose (*Rosa*) (for love)
- 1 tablespoon (15 ml) jasmine (*Jasminum officinale*) (for love)
- 1 tablespoon (15 ml) lavender (*Lavandula angustifolia*) (for love)
- 1 pinch crossroads dirt (for love, power)
- Lighter or matches

WORKING

1. Use the pin, needle, or knife to carve the word "Love" into the candle.

2. Set the candleholder on the plate. Place the candle in the holder.

3. Sprinkle the herbs around the candle.

4. Sprinkle the crossroads dirt over the herbs.

5. Light the candle. State:

   Candlelight, burn bright. Bring love through this magical rite.

6. Let the candle burn for 10 minutes, then extinguish it.

7. Light the candle daily, and let it burn for 10 minutes. Every time you light the candle, state:

   Candlelight, burn bright. Bring love through this magical rite.

8. Once the candle has burned out, dispose of the materials in the trash.

LUST FOR ME NOW CHARM BAG

This spell will attract lust to your life. Your personal lust will increase—as will the lust other people have toward you.

MATERIALS

- Small red drawstring bag
- 3 small carnelian tumbles (for lust)

- 2 tablespoons (30 ml) cardamom (*Elettaria cardamomum*) (for lust)
- 4 tablespoons (60 ml) crossroads dirt (for love, power)
- 1 tablespoon (15 ml) patchouli leaf (*Pogostemon cablin*) (for desire, lust)
- ½ tablespoon (7.5 ml) cayenne pepper (*Capsicum annuum*) (for heat, power, speed)
- 20-inch (51-cm) necklace chain
- ¼ cup (60 ml) cherry juice (*Prunus avium*) (for lust)
- Paintbrush

WORKING

1. Place the tumbles, herbal materials, and dirt in the bag one at a time. As you add each item to the bag, feel and sense lustful energy growing inside it. Know that your own sexual desires are rising and that your need for attention is growing.

2. Pull the drawstring bag closed and attach the necklace chain to it.

3. Dip the paintbrush in the cherry juice, and paint the juice over the bag, anointing the bag with it.

4. When you go out on the town and to the clubs looking for a date and a night of casual and lustful fun, wear the charm bag. The chain should be long enough for the bag to hang about the center of your chest.

5. Anoint the charm bag with cherry juice every time you go out with it. Anoint and wear the bag

for as long as you feel the need for a boost in lust and desire.

6. When you no longer need the charm, dispose of the dirt and herbs as you see fit. The carnelian tumbles can be cleansed and used in other work. The bag can be washed and used in other magical work too.

Protection & Removal through Crossroads Dirt

Crossroads are powerful locations. The energy they have reaches across the various worlds and realities. This energy can be utilized to aid you in protecting yourself against entities that exist in any time, space, or reality. From ghosts and apparitions to elemental spirits and other beings, no matter what realm they come from, crossroads dirt can be used to protect you from them if you don't want them around. Along with spirits, crossroads dirt can be used to protect ourselves against mundane harm as well as magical and spiritual attacks.

CROSSROADS BINDING

Sometimes we just need to bind someone from causing harm for a while.

This and other binding spells should be used before trying a hex or curse to deal with the situation but after other magical and mundane efforts have been tried.

MATERIALS

- 9.75-by-7.5-inch (25-by-19-cm) piece of paper
- Pen
- 1 tablespoon (15 ml) crossroads dirt (for binding, protection)
- 3-to-5-inch (7.5-to-13-cm) length of a fresh ivy plant (*Hedera helix*) (for binding)
- Scissors
- 20 inches (51 cm) black ribbon

WORKING

1. On the paper, write your target's name and date of birth five times. If that information is unknown, write a descriptive statement that identifies the target five times.

2. Rotate the paper 90 degrees and write "Bound from Causing Harm" five times across the name and birthdate or identifying information.

3. Scatter the crossroads dirt over the written information. As you sprinkle the dirt, state:

   No matter where you are found, your fate is to be bound.

4. Fold the paper in half, folding away from yourself.

5. Cut the ivy in half. Wrap one half around the packet and tie it tight. Rotate the packet 90 degrees and tie the other half of the ivy around the packet, making a cross with the ivy strands. As you tie the second ivy strand, state:

> *By the power of this ivy vine, the trouble*
> *you have caused places you in this bind.*

6. Wrap the black ribbon around the packet until it is completely covered. As you wrap, repeat the following chant:

> *I bind you this day from harm that you have*
> *done. Going forward you are a danger to*
> *none.*

7. Place the packet somewhere it will not be disturbed. Leave the packet there until the problem has been addressed or solved.

8. When you are confident your target will not harm another person intentionally, use the scissors to cut the ribbon and ivy to open and unseal the packet. Once the packet has been unsealed, the bound individual is released. Dispose of the packet and all it contains in the trash.

TO SEND AWAY REMOVAL SPELL

Removing that which is unwanted is a powerful way to bring change to your life with crossroads dirt. This spell works to send people and forces away from you and your loved ones.

For safety reasons, perform this spell outside and away from flammable debris.

MATERIALS
- Pen
- Paper
- Firesafe bowl

- Lighter or matches
- 2 tablespoons (30 ml) crossroads dirt (for protection, removal, reversal)
- ½ tablespoon (7.5 ml) cayenne pepper (*Capsicum annuum*) (for removal, speed)
- Fire extinguisher or bucket of water

WORKING

1. Clear your outdoor workspace of any flammable debris. Set the fire extinguisher or bucket of water nearby.

2. On the paper, write out what you want sent away and removed from your life. This can be a person, behavior, or other force that you want—and need—out of your life. As you write out these things, state:

   (Insert what's being removed) be gone.

3. Tear the paper into small pieces. As you rip the paper, direct your desire to have those forces removed from your life into the paper. Toss the pieces into the firesafe bowl.

4. Light the paper on fire. Let the paper burn completely and turn to ash.

5. Once the ash has cooled, use your hands to mix the crossroads dirt and cayenne pepper in with the ash. As you mix the materials together, state:

   (Insert what's being removed) be gone.

6. Take the mixture to the end of your driveway or parking lot. If possible, go down your road. Sprinkle the dirt away from your home. Know that as people drive over the mixture, what you want removed from your life will be sent away.

Crossroads Baneful Magic

Crossroads dirt is an excellent tool for baneful magic, and there are many people who immediately think about baneful magic when they consider working with the dirt. There are many trickster spirits associated with crossroads. For this reason, it is not unreasonable to associate crossroads dirt with baneful magic.

As with all baneful magic, think carefully about the potential consequences of your actions before performing the work.

REAP WHAT YOU SOW SPELL

Use this spell to cause your target to reap the results of all the problems they have caused other people. This spell not only returns what the individual has sent out to others but adds your pain to it, giving them a double dose of justice.

The two mirrors need to be able to stand on their own. Desk- or dresser top–sized is best.

MATERIALS
- 2 9.75-by-7.5-inch (25-by-19-cm) pieces of paper
- Pen

- Small black candle
- Pin, needle, or knife
- Paper
- 2 tablespoons (30 ml) crossroads dirt (for baneful magic, cursing)
- 2 tablespoons (30 ml) ground black peppercorn (*Piper nigrum*) (to return to sender and for baneful magic, reversal)
- 2 tablespoons (30 ml) stinging nettle (*Urtica dioica*) (to return to sender and for baneful magic, reversal)
- 2 tablespoons (30 ml) ground galangal root (*Alpinia galanga*) (to return to sender and for baneful magic, reversal)
- Candleholder
- 2 mirrors
- Lighter or matches

WORKING

1. On one sheet of paper, draw a sigil that combines the symbols for the planets Saturn and Pluto.

$$\hbar \quad P$$

   Take your time creating the sigil. The more time and effort you put into designing the symbol, the more power it will have.

2. Use the pin, needle, or knife to carve the symbol you created into one side of the candle. As you carve this sigil, state:

> *To (target's name) does their actions
> return, until this lesson they do learn.*

3. On the second piece of paper, draw the planetary symbols.

4. Sprinkle the crossroads dirt and herbal materials along the lines of the planetary symbols one at a time. As you sprinkle each material, state:

> *To reflect back and make (target's name)'s
> actions become an attack.*

5. Set the candleholder on top of the dirt and herbal materials. Place the candle in the holder.

6. Place the two mirrors across from one another so they reflect off each other. The candle should be between them.

7. Light the candle, stating:

> *As this candle does burn, a cosmic lesson
> for (target's name) to learn. To them, may
> all they sent return.*

8. Let the candle burn out. Once the candle has finished burning, dispose of the candle, herbs, dirt, and paper in a trash can away from your home. The mirrors can be cleansed and used again in other magical works.

TO MAKE SOMEONE LOST CURSE

This spell is for when you need to have someone get lost. The spell works with becoming physically lost, as well as being lost mentally without any meaning or direction in life.

MATERIALS

- Pen
- Slip of paper
- 2 small toy mazes
- Scissors
- 1 to 3 pinches crossroads dirt (to make someone lost and confused)
- 1 tablespoon (15 ml) poppy seeds (*Papaver somniferum*) (for chaos, confusion)
- 1 tablespoon (15 ml) cayenne pepper (*Capsicum annuum*) (for baneful magic, heat, speed)
- Hot glue gun and glue

WORKING

1. On the slip of paper, write out your target's name. If your target's name is unknown, write down a way that they can be identified.

2. Turn one of the pocket mazes over so the maze faces the floor and the backing faces you. Place the slip of paper on top of the maze.

3. Sprinkle the crossroads dirt over the slip of paper. As you sprinkle the dirt, state:

    To make (target's name) lost and confused.

4. Sprinkle the poppy seed over your target's name. State:

    For chaos and confusion.

5. Sprinkle the cayenne pepper over the seeds and dirt. State:

   For heat and speed.

6. Apply glue to the back of the second maze. Stick the two mazes back-to-back so the paper, dirt, seeds, and pepper are between them.

7. Set the maze sandwich aside so the glue can dry.

8. Once the glue has dried, begin playing with the mazes. The more you play with them, the more lost and confused your target will become.

9. Once you feel that your target has learned their lesson, pull the two mazes apart and dispose of the herbs, dirt, and paper in a trash can away from your home and place of work. The mazes can be used in other magical works.

CEMETERIES &
GRAVEYARDS

I f there is one type of dirt that is almost always associated with magic and witchcraft, it is that of cemetery and graveyard dirt. In Conjure, as well as many Traditional Witchcraft practices, before any spirits are called into the ritual, the ancestors are called first. Even ancestors whose names are unknown will come to help magical work. All a person needs to do to call on their power is add a pinch of cemetery or graveyard dirt to their spell.

Working with cemetery dirt is not something I would recommend for beginners. Before attempting to harvest cemetery dirt, work with your ancestors first. Like crossroads dirt, working with cemetery dirt requires some extra preparation.

Myths & Misconceptions

This type of dirt is surrounded by myths and misconceptions. These beliefs often lead to fear of working with this dirt. Here are some of the myths and misconceptions about cemetery and graveyard dirt and the facts behind them.

Myth: "Cemetery" and "graveyard" are interchangeable words.
Truth: That myth is partially correct. Both terms refer to places where the remains of the dead are placed to rest. Graveyards are tied to churches; they are the plots of land behind churches where members can be buried. Cemeteries are not owned by any church or religious organization. The only requirement to be buried there is to buy the burial plot. You can also bury ashes in a cemetery but not in a graveyard.

When it comes to magical and spiritual work, cemetery and graveyard dirt can be used the same ways. This is why you often find the words used interchangeably. Going forward, I will use the word "cemetery."

Myth: "Cemetery dirt" typically refers to the herb patchouli (*Pogostemon cablin*).
Truth: "Cemetery dirt" is one of the many folk names for patchouli. While some recipes and workings refer to patchouli when they use the term, in many magical traditions and practices, the term "cemetery dirt" means exactly that—dirt from cemeteries and graveyards.

Myth: Cemetery dirt can only be gathered at night.
Truth: Traditionally cemetery dirt is gathered at night. However, many cemeteries and graveyards have hours of operation that are only during the day. In this case, gathering the dirt at night would be considered trespassing and be illegal. You can gather the dirt during the day.

Myth: Cemetery dirt is only used for baneful magic (curses and hexes).
Truth: While cemetery dirt is a powerful tool in baneful magic, it can be used for many other things. Healing and protection are two common uses. You can use the dirt for necromancy workings (workings with the dead) too. It can also be added to any spell to call on your ancestors and ask them to empower your spell.

Myth: Cemetery dirt has to be taken from graves only.
Truth: When there is no connection to anyone laid to rest in the cemetery, you can work with dirt from the cemetery in general. Just gather dirt from one of the walkways or paths instead. You will still need to do all of the spiritual prep before gathering any of the dirt.

Myth: Working with cemetery dirt is dangerous.
Truth: There is some danger, but it most often comes from when the dirt is gathered disrespectfully. If you respect and honor the spirits of the cemetery, as well any person whose grave you may harvest the dirt from, you have nothing to

worry about. As long as you are respectful and have wards and protections in place, no unwanted spirit or danger can come to you.

Another danger comes from working with dirt harvested from the grave of someone that you did not know. It is always best to work with people that you knew or had a direct connection to while they were alive. If you gather dirt from an unknown individual, you have no idea what kind of person they were in life. Dying and living in the world of the spirits does not mean that they are a good and helpful person, and you cannot trust that an unknown spirit won't take your work and turn it against you for their own amusement. Of course, even your own ancestors could do this. If they were a problematic individual during their life, they are going to be the same in death. Death does not change a person's spirit or personality.

On a mundane note, taking dirt from a stranger's grave is unethical. When you work with dirt from a stranger's grave, you risk upsetting the individual's loved ones. You'd also be stealing from the spirit of the dead. It is also illegal. Do not break the law just to gather dirt.

Myth: Once you are dead and in the spirit world, you have greater knowledge and wisdom than you did in life. You can now know anything you want to know.

Truth: While the dead may have some greater insight into the past and future (linear time does not exist in the spirit world), they are not all knowing or wise. They are simply the same person they were in life. Anything that you would have asked them for advice about in life, they can still help you with in death. If it's nothing they would have known about while alive, they still won't know anything about it in death.

Myth: Spirits from the cemetery will follow you home.
Truth: When you perform magic and spiritual acts, such as gathering cemetery dirt, you do get the attention of spirits. Most of these spirits are merely curious about you and what you are doing. Occasionally you may find a spirit that has baneful intent toward you—or people in general. This is why it is important to have protection charms and to cleanse yourself before and after visiting the cemetery.

Preparation

Now that some of the myths have been covered, it is time to talk about the work to be done before you can harvest and use cemetery dirt. The two main things that need to be done are cleansing and establishing protection. You need to cleanse yourself before you enter and after you leave the cemetery and have protection from unwanted spirits.

CLEANSE & NEUTRALIZE BATH

Cleansing your spirit before entering the cemetery is important. Not all of the spirits within a cemetery are going to be resting peacefully. If you have negative energy on or around you, restless spirits may find you and cause trouble in your life. Removal of that energy prevents this from happening.

Showers and baths are best for cleansing work. The water removes all of the unwanted energy, sending it down the drain. When showers and baths are not an option, I like to anoint myself with oils or colognes. Most colognes can both protect and cleanse, making them perfect tools for magic on the go. The resource section has a few formulas for these colognes.

If bathing is an option, use this working to cleanse and neutralize energetic forces in your life.

MATERIALS
- Mortar and pestle
- Small bowl
- Spoon or wand
- 2 teaspoons (10 ml) sea salt (to absorb, cleanse, neutralize)
- 1 teaspoon (5 ml) wood betony (*Pedicularis canadensis*) (for protection, purification)
- 1 teaspoon (5 ml) elder flower or elder berry (*Sambucus nigra*) (for exorcism, protection)
- ½ teaspoon (2.5 ml) galangal root (*Alpinia galanga*) (for banishment, exorcism, removal)
- ½ teaspoon (2.5 ml) hyssop (*Hyssopus officinalis*) (for cleaning, protection, purification)
- Cheesecloth

- Kitchen twine
- Bath towel

WORKING

1. Use the mortar and pestle to grind each of the herbs into as fine of a powder as you possibly can, then transfer each powder to the bowl. As you grind each of the herbs, state what you are using them for and thank the spirits of the herbs for their help in this work.

2. Once all of the herbs are ground and in the bowl, use the spoon or wand to mix them together. As you stir, repeat the following chant until the herbs are thoroughly mixed, about five to seven times:

    Cleanse and clean today. Remove all negativity that stands in my way.

3. Transfer the herbal mixture from the bowl to the center of the cheesecloth.

4. Bundle up the cheesecloth and use the twine to secure it. If you are taking a bath, set the cheesecloth sachet in the tub and run the water. If you are working with a shower, tie the bundle around the showerhead before turning it on.

5. Wash your body from head to toe using soap as well as the herbal-infused water.

6. As you leave the bath or shower, pat yourself dry with the towel. The patting of the towel will seal in the energetic cleanse and the protection.

Dispose of the bundle by burying the herbs in the ground if possible. When burial of the herbs is not possible, respectfully dispose of them in the trash.

ROWAN PROTECTION SACHET

While cleansing will remove any negative and unwanted energy from you, restless spirits may still try to cause problems in your life. This is why it is essential to have a protective charm of some sort on you. These charms will repel evil and protect you from spirits with ill intentions. Jewelry and other items that can be worn serve as excellent protection charms. If you don't wear or own jewelry, protection sachets can be made and carried with you.

Use this working to create a simple sachet that will keep you safe from witchcraft, baneful energy, and any spirits or forces that would wish you harm.

MATERIALS
- Small black drawstring bag
- 5 rowan thorns (*Sorbus aucuparia*) (for protection against evil, spirits, and witchcraft)
- 3 dried blackberries (*Rubus*) (for protection from spirits)
- 1 tablespoon (15 ml) arnica flowers (*Arnica montana*) (for protection from spirits)
- Obsidian stone (for protection)
- 1 tablespoon (15 ml) yarrow (*Achillea millefolium*) (for protection from spirits)

WORKING

1. Place half of the rowan thorns in the bag. As you add the thorns, state:

   Thorns from the rowan tree, keep all spirits with ill intent away from me.

2. Add the blackberries to the bag. As you place each of the berries in the bag, state:

   Summer-sweet blackberry, keep evil spirits away from me.

3. Place the arnica flowers in the bag. As you add them, state:

   Flowers of the arnica plant, provide protection where the others can't.

4. Add the obsidian stone to the bag, stating:

   Obsidian, volcanic ash stone, protect me from spirits that are unknown.

5. Add the yarrow flowers to the bag. As you add the flowers, state:

   Flower of yarrow, yellow and bright, keep evil away from me with this rite.

6. Pull the bag closed and use your hands to play with it. As you play with the bag, feel the power of the materials inside surround you and create an energetic force field that will protect you from all that would wish you harm.

7. Carry the sachet with you. When you feel the need for the extra protection hold the bag in

your hands and play with it. That will activate its energy and provide you with protection.

Guardian of the Cemetery

The last thing to consider before working with cemetery dirt is the guardian spirit of the cemetery. This spirit is a combination of the land as well as everyone who is buried there. The job of this spirit is to protect the dead from being disturbed.

When you are going to gather cemetery dirt, a small offering needs to be given to the guardian spirit. This offering shows that you acknowledge the spirit and respect the dead. A small bit of water is all you need to offer. Simply pour a little out at the entrance and say it's for the guardian of the cemetery. Once the offering has been given, you can go to the spot you are going to gather the dirt from.

Gathering Cemetery Dirt

There are two types of cemetery dirt. First, you have the dirt that comes from a specific grave. That dirt can be used to call upon that specific individual as well as the powers of the dead in general. The second type is pure cemetery dirt. Pure cemetery dirt is dirt that just contains the power and essence of the cemetery. This dirt can be gathered from the entrances to cemeteries as well as from the roads and walking paths within them.

The best way to gather cemetery dirt from a specific grave is to gather the dirt around the headstone or marker. Being in the ground, a marker always has the chance of getting dirty, and between weather and the passing of time, dirt will find its way onto it. Gathering dirt this way can be looked at as an act of cleaning the grave. After the grave has been cleaned, leave an offering of thanks (flowers or water) and payment for the dirt.

Unless you have a reason to call on a specific ancestor, it is best to use pure cemetery dirt. When you gather dirt from a specific grave, you can disrupt the grave. Other loved ones of that individual, including your own relatives, might not be happy about a disrupted grave. Staying away from direct burial sites and gathering dirt from paths within the cemetery prevents you from disturbing the grave.

GATHERING CEMETERY DIRT

The process of gathering cemetery dirt is fairly simple. Like with other dirt, it is important to give an offering to the spirits of the location. As there are spirits of the dead as well as the guardian spirit, payment for dirt must be made before and after the dirt is gathered. Remember to cleanse yourself and have a protection charm of some sort on you.

MATERIALS
- Bottle of water
- Miniature broom

- Small plastic baggie
- Coin or flowers

WORKING

1. Upon entering the cemetery, pour a small offering of water out to the guardian spirit. State your name and why you are there.

2. Travel to where you are going to gather the dirt. If you are gathering dirt from a grave site, pour out another offering of water. If gathering general dirt, there is no need to give a second offering yet.

3. Use the miniature broom to brush some dirt into the plastic baggie.

4. Once you have gathered the dirt you need, place the coin on the ground and thank the spirit for the dirt. If you brought flowers, place the flowers according to the rules of the cemetery.

5. Return home. If possible, leave by a different road to confuse any spirits that may want to follow you. Cleanse yourself when you return home.

Working with Ancestors & the Dead

Cemetery dirt is primarily used to work with ancestral spirits and the spirits of the dead. Ancestor spirits come in two main forms: your blood ancestors and the ancestors of your heart. Blood ancestors will always be your ancestors, even if you have no emotional connection to them or knowledge of them. Your blood provides the connection. Ancestors of the heart are those that are chosen family. You may have no direct biological connection, but when it comes to the heart and spirit, they are people you cherish and consider family. Pets, friends, mentors, and other relationships of this sort are part of your ancestors of the heart.

When you gather dirt from the graves of your loved ones, that dirt can be used for any ancestral work you want to do. It can be used to create a spirit vessel for your ancestors, or it can simply be used as a tool to connect with them and ask for their help in spells or ritual work. The important thing is that the dirt provides a physical representation of your ancestors.

ANCESTOR SKULL SPIRIT HOME RITUAL

Ancestor veneration is a large part of Conjure and Traditional Witchcraft. One of the tools to aid in ancestor veneration is that of the skull spirit home. Using a fake skull and cemetery dirt, you can create a place on your altar for your ancestors to stay when they visit you.

Try to find a ceramic, porcelain, or clay skull. They work best. A crystal skull will also work. The recipe for underworld incense can be found in part 3.

MATERIALS

- Altar
- Altar cloth
- Small fake skull
- Small bowl of cemetery dirt
- Heat pad
- Censer
- Charcoal disc
- Long-stemmed lighter
- 2 tablespoons (30 ml) underworld incense
- Black candle
- Candleholder
- Bowl of water

WORKING

1. Begin by setting up the altar. Place the skull in the center. In the back, facing the north, place the bowl of cemetery dirt. Put the candle in its holder and place it in the east. Set the censer and heat pad in the south and the bowl of water in the west.

2. Use the tongs to hold the charcoal disc and light the disc. Once the disc begins to glow and spark, carefully place it in the censer.

3. Sprinkle the incense over the charcoal. Let it smolder.

4. Light the candle.

5. Walk the perimeter of your ritual circle widdershins (counterclockwise) three times. As you walk, feel yourself traveling into the underworld.

6. When you return to the altar after the third rotation, tap the ground three times and the sky three times. Stand in the center of the altar.

7. Raise the skull above your head and state:

   I call upon the powers of my ancestors. Be here today to bless this skull that it may be a home for you during rituals. That you may always have a home in my home. Blessed ancestors, I bid thee hail and welcome.

8. Place the skull back on the altar. Pick up the bowl of cemetery dirt. Rub some of the dirt into the skull. As you do so, state:

   I bless this skull with the power of the earth, which provides form.

9. Set the bowl down and pick up the skull. Pass it over the candle flame. As you do so, state:

   I bless this skull with the power of fire, the passion and spark of life.

10. Pass the skull through the incense smoke. As you do so, state:

    I bless this skull with the power of air, the breath of life.

11. Using your hand as a cup, anoint the skull with the water. As you rub the water into the skull, state:

    I bless this skull with the power of water, our blood and emotions.

12. Set the skull back in the center of the altar.

13. Stand in front of the altar and place your hands over the skull. State:

    > *By the power of the elements, may this skull provide a home for my ancestral spirits. May they have this place of rest and honor.*

14. Sit in front of the altar and think about your ancestors. Thank them for what they have given you. Know that they will always be with you.

15. When you are done talking with your ancestors, extinguish the incense and candle.

16. Walk the perimeter of the circle three times desoil (clockwise). As you walk, know that you have returned to this middle world and the portal has been closed. When the censer and candle have cooled, return them to storage. Place the skull on your main altar or where you can see it and it will not be disturbed.

To Bring in Romance Candle Spell

Use this spell to attract someone to be your partner in life. The individual will be a romantic, sexual, and general life partner to you.

When gathering supplies, try to find tea light candles that have a cinnamon scent.

MATERIALS
- Dinner plate
- Red pillar candle

- Pin, needle, or knife
- 4 red tea light candles
- 4 tea light candleholders
- 1 tablespoon (15 ml) sugar (for attraction)
- 2 pinches red rose petals (*Rosa*) (for love)
- 1 pinch jasmine (*Jasminum officinale*) (for love)
- 1 pinch catnip (*Nepeta cataria*) (for happiness, love)
- 1 teaspoon (5 ml) cinnamon (*Cinnamomum verum*) (for desire, love, lust passion)
- 2 pinches cemetery dirt (to call on your ancestors)
- Lighter or matches

WORKING

1. Use the pin, needle, or knife to carve the word "Partner," "Husband," or "Wife" into the pillar candle. Use whatever term best describes the relationship you are looking for.

2. Set the pillar candle in the center of the plate.

3. Place the four tea light candles in their holders and position them around the plate to represent the four cardinal directions.

4. Sprinkle the sugar around the pillar candle. State:

   Sugar that is sweet, a partner I would like to meet.

5. Lay the rose petals down over the sugar. State:

   Red rose for a love that is new and a love that is true.

6. Sprinkle the jasmine over the rose petals. State:

   Jasmine for love that will honor me and see me for me.

7. Sprinkle the catnip over the jasmine. State:

   Catnip for happiness and love.

8. Sprinkle the cinnamon over the catnip. State:

   Cinnamon for a partner to love me and desire me.

9. Sprinkle the cemetery dirt over the cinnamon. State:

   Ancestors of mine, I call upon you today to send the perfect partner my way.

10. Light the candles. State:

    Candle that is burning bright, love, passion, and desire from a partner I seek tonight.

11. Let the candles burn for 10 minutes. After 10 minutes, extinguish the flames.

12. For the next several days, burn the candles for 10 minutes until they have completely burned. Let the wax from the candles naturally fall onto the plate and over the herbs and sugar. Once the candles have fully burned, dispose of them in the trash. If possible, dispose of the herbs by burial. If burial is not practical or possible, then you can simply thank the herbs for their work and dispose of them respectfully in the trash

INTERVIEW COURAGE CHARM

Job interviews can be nerve-racking. This spell creates a small charm you can carry with you when you go to a job interview. It will help you show your best self.

MATERIALS
- Yellow paint
- 2 small paper plates
- Small wooden disc or coin
- Paintbrush
- ½ teaspoon (2.5 ml) cemetery dirt (for ancestral aid)
- 1 teaspoon (5 ml) plantain (*Plantago major*) (for courage, strength)
- 1 teaspoon (5 ml) yellow dock (*Rumex crispus*) (for money)
- Pen
- Paper
- Paintbrush
- Green paint
- Glass of water
- Paper towels

WORKING
1. Squirt or pour some yellow paint on a paper plate.

2. Add the dirt and herbs to the second plate. Use your hands to mix them together. As you mix the materials, focus on acing the job interview and getting the job you want. Direct that energy into the mixture. Push the mixture into a pile, then divide that pile into four.

3. Add one dirt and herb pile to the yellow paint. Use the paintbrush to stir the dirt and herbs into

the paint. As you do so, repeat the following mantra three to five times:

> *Being confident and strong brings a new job along.*

4. Paint one side of the disc or coin yellow. Set the coin aside to dry. Clean your paintbrush using the water and paper towels.

5. While the paint dries, use the pen and paper to draft two sigils. One sigil should use the symbols for Jupiter, Mercury, and Mars, and the other sigil should use the symbols for Venus, Mars, and Jupiter.

6. Once the coin is dry, pour some green paint onto the paper plate. Mix another pile of dirt into the paint. While mixing the paint, repeat the following mantra three to five times:

> *Confidence they shall see. Employed I will be.*

7. Paint one of the two sigils on the coin. While you paint, focus on feeling confident during your interview. See yourself being employed. Direct that energy into the sigil.

8. Set the coin aside to dry.

9. Once that side of the coin has dried, flip the coin over and repeat steps 4 through 7 using the

remaining dirt and herbs, fresh paint, and the second sigil.

10. Again, set the coin aside to dry. As it does, dispose of paper plates and paint water appropriately.

11. Carry the coin with you when you have the job interview. While you are waiting for the interview, fiddle with the coin and let its energy flow into you. You will do fine.

12. When you get a job, thank your ancestors. If possible, burn the coin to release the energy back to the universe. Otherwise, respectfully dispose of the coin by burying it or placing it in nature, allowing it to decompose naturally. Disposal in the trash is recommended only when no other options are available.

HEALING BOWL SPELL

Everyone is capable of sending healing energy, and our ancestors are no different. Asking our ancestors for healing adds substantial power to our spells, especially if our loved one died of a terrible illness.

This spell needs to be recast once a month. New names can be added each time the spell is cast.

MATERIALS
- Pen
- Paper
- Scissors

- Large bowl
- Pillar candleholder
- Blue pillar candle
- 2 tablespoons (30 ml) lavender (*Lavandula angustifolia*) (for healing)
- 3 amethyst tumbles (for healing)
- 1 tablespoon (15 ml) marigold (*Calendula officinalis*) (for healing)
- 3 rose quartz tumbles (healing, love, relationships with family and friends)
- 1 tablespoon (15 ml) allheal (*Prunella vulgaris*) (for healing)
- 3 lapis lazuli tumbles (for healing)
- 1 tablespoon (15 ml) angelica root (*Angelica archangelica*) (for healing)
- 3 howlite tumbles (for healing)
- 1 tablespoon (15 ml) chamomile (*Matricaria recutita*) (for healing)
- 3 tablespoons (45 ml) cemetery dirt (for ancestral aid in healing)
- Lighter or matches

WORKING

1. On the paper, list the names of your family members or loved ones that need healing.

2. Cut the paper into strips. Each name should be on its own slip.

3. Place the slips of paper in the bowl.

4. Set the candleholder on top of the paper and place the candle in the holder.

5. Sprinkle the lavender around the candle. Try to lay them out as evenly as possible. As you place the lavender, state:

   For healing power.

6. Place the amethyst in the bowl so the candle is in the middle of a crystal triangle. As you place each amethyst, state:

   For healing power.

7. Lay the marigold down around the candle. State:

   For healing power.

8. Place a rose quartz next to each of the amethyst tumbles. As you place each tumble, state:

   For healing power.

9. Sprinkle the allheal around the candle. State:

   For healing power.

10. Place the lapis lazuli next to the rose quartz. As you place each tumble, state:

    For healing power.

11. Lay the angelica root over the other herbs. State:

    To heal those in need.

12. Set the howlite next to the lapis lazuli. As you place each tumble, state:

    For healing power.

13. Lay the chamomile over the other herbs. State:

    For peace, calm, and healing.

14. Sprinkle the cemetery dirt around the candle and over the herbs and crystals. As you do so, state:

    I call upon the power of my ancestors tonight. May you aid me in healing my family and loved one through this rite.

15. Place your hands over the bowl. Feel a light blue healing energy pulsate from your hands and flow into the bowl, covering all of the materials with its light. State:

    Healing power to those whose names are here. Let this healing light reach those in need through this rite.

16. Light the candle and let it burn for 5 minutes. After 5 minutes, extinguish the candle.

17. For the next month, repeat steps 15 and 16 daily. If the candle finishes burning before the end of the month, get a new candle.

18. At the end of the month, take the bowl apart. Toss all of the slips of paper in the trash. Dispose of the herbs by burial in the earth. When that is not possible, thank the herbs for their help and respectfully dispose of them in the trash.

PART III
RESOURCES

LOCATION
CORRESPONDENCES

T here were many locations covered in this text. This comprehensive list covers all of the types of dirt and locations listed in the text as well as additional locations that were not covered in the text.

Bank/Credit Union/Financial Institution: Financial security, financial stability, money

Bar/Night Club: Dating, healing alcoholism, love, lust, passion, relationships, sexuality, targeting an alcoholic

Beauty Salon: Beauty, love, relationships, self-esteem, self-love, stopping gossip

Casino: Bad luck, good luck, healing gambling addictions, money, prosperity, success

Cemetery/Graveyard: Ancestral work, working with the dead, underworld work

Church Dirt: Blessing, power of the church's deity, prayer power, protection

Crossroads: Dispersing energy, powering spells, spirit work, spirit world travels

Courthouse Dirt: Justice, legal issues, protection

Desert: Baneful magic, speed, strength, survival

Doctor's Office/Hospital: Causing illness, healing, health

Forest: Creating an otherworldly gate, fear, fertility, nightmares, protection, prosperity

Garden: Growth, personal effect of the garden, personal effect of the garden owner

Home: Family, home, household issues, impacting house/home, personal effect of the individuals living within the building

Library/School/Training Center: Block busting, knowledge, memory, opening roads, wisdom

Liquor Store: Healing alcoholism, targeting an alcoholic

Mall/Shopping Center: Dating, love, luck, money, prosperity, relationships, success

Massage Parlor/Spa: Beauty, healing, self-care, self-love, stress relief

Mental Health Clinic: Healing, impacting mental health, mental health aid, mental health relief

Mountain: Creating blocks, divination, protection, psychic sight, spirituality

Ocean: Attraction, cleansing, commerce, money

Police Station: Baneful magic, justice, protection

River/Stream: Attraction, bogging someone down, cleansing, removal

Shipping Center/Transportation Center: Attracting business, moving things, removal, travel

Stop Sign: Freezing work, making things stop, stopping gossip

Swamp: Fear, protection, underworld work, working with the dead, working with spirit realms

Tides: Change, chaos, confusion, power

Volcano: Block busting, opening roads, protection, removal, stress relief

Work Place: Career work, employment, money, personal effect of where you work

ANIMAL CORRESPONDENCES

There are many more animals than those mentioned in the "Animal Tracks" chapter. This list covers the animals mentioned there plus many others. While extensive, this list is by no means complete. Refer back to the "Animal Tracks" chapter for help establishing correspondences for any animals not listed here.

Alligators: Hiding in plain sight, luck, opportunities, patience

Ant Hills: Adaptability, block busting, overcoming obstacles, road opening, stability

Bears: Protection, road opening, strength

Beavers: Camouflage, construction of homes and buildings, plugging up the works

Cats: Magic power, psychic gifts and abilities, shape-shifting, spirit work

Chickens: Cleansing, protection, removal

Cougars: Beauty, cunning, elegance, power, speed, strength

Cows: Abundance, fertility, motherhood

Coyotes: Attraction, cunning, luck

Deer: Beauty, camouflage, elegance, Horned God of Wicca, speed

Dogs: Friendship, honest emotions, loyalty, protection, socialization

Fire Ant Hills: Baneful Magic, pain, protection

Foxes: Beauty, cunning, intelligence, lust, sexuality, trickery

Goats: Resilience, stubbornness, versatility

Horses: Creativity, healing, health, intelligence, luck, speed

Mice: Adaptability, charm, criticism, survival

Rabbits: Fertility, good luck, prosperity, speed, success

Sheep: Creativity, innocence, renewal

Snails: Causing a pause, slowing things down

Snakes: Baneful magic, luck, new beginnings, wisdom

Squirrels: Industriousness, planning, prosperity

Termite Mounds: Baneful magic, decay, destruction, justice, revenge

Wolves: Fear, intimidation, intuition, loyalty, shape-shifting, spirituality, wisdom

HERB, ROOT & FLOWER CORRESPONDENCES

This is a complete list of all the herbal or plant matter that can be found in this text. As always, use these correspondences as a starting point. May this list inspire your spell-crafting creativity.

Acorn (*Quercus robur*): Fertility, masculinity, power, strength

Alfalfa (*Medicago sativa*): Fertility, prosperity, success

Allheal (*Prunella vulgaris*): Healing, protection against illness

Allspice (*Pimenta dioica*): Luck, money, prosperity

Apple (*Malus domestica*): Attraction, fertility, money, prosperity, success, underworld work

Angelica (*Angelica archangelica*): Angelic work, banishing, blessing, healing, protection, removal

Arnica (*Arnica montana*): Healing, pain relief, protection

Avocado (*Persea americana*): Fertility

Banana (*Musa acuminata, Musa balbisiana*): Fertility

Basil (*Ocimum basilicum*): Attracting spirits, block busting, good luck, road opening, sacred to Yahweh, spirit realms, underworld work, working with the dead

Bay (*Laurus nobilis*): Block busting, road opening, strength

Beet (*Beta vulgaris*): Love, relationships, romance

Bilberry (*Vaccinium myrtillus*): Attracting luck, money, protection, success, wealth

Birch (*Betula pendula*): Banishing, healing, protection, protection against baneful magic, removal

Blackberry (*Rubus*): Money, luck, protection, removal, reversal, success

Black Peppercorn (*Piper nigrum*): Baneful magic, banishing, protection, removal, reversal

Cardamom (*Elettaria cardamomum*): Lust

Carrot (*Daucus carota*): Divination, psychic sight, spirit work, underworld work

Catnip (*Nepeta cataria*): Dating, friendship, happiness

Cayenne Pepper (*Capsicum annuum*): Banishment, causing pain, cursing/hexing, hex breaking, justice, protection, removal, reversal

Chamomile (*Matricaria recutita*): Happiness, home, love, mental focus, peace, sweetening

Cherry (*Prunus avium*): Lust, passion, relationships, sexuality

Cinquefoil (*Potentilla simplex*): Fast cash

Cinnamon (*Cinnamomum verum*): Attraction, employment, good luck, love, lust, money, prosperity, sexuality

Clove (*Syzygium aromaticum*): Good luck

Clover (*Trifolium repens*): Beauty, good luck, love

Coriander (*Coriandrum sativum*): Healing, lust

Damiana (*Turnera diffusa*): Meditation, psychic sight, spirituality, trance work

Dandelion (*Taraxacum officinale*): Money, power, wealth, wishes

Devil's Shoestring (*Viburnum alnifolium*): Ensnaring baneful magic, protection from evil

Dragon's Blood (*Dracaena cinnabari*): Money, protection

Elder (*Sambucus nigra*): Protection, protection against baneful magic, return, reversal

Eucalyptus (*Eucalyptus* sp.): Cleansing, healing

Eyebright (*Euphrasia rostkoviana*): Divination, psychic sight, spirit communication, spirit work

Feverfew (*Tanacetum parthenium*): Protection from and wards against illness

Frankincense (*Boswellia sacra*): Blessing, cleansing, meditation, protection, psychic abilities, sacred to Yahweh, spirituality

Galangal (*Alpinia galanga*): Baneful magic, cursing, heating up, hex breaking, justice, protection, removal, reversal

Ginger (*Zingiber officinale*): Justice, protection, returning to sender

Ginkgo (*Ginkgo biloba*): Healing, mental focus, mental powers, opening the mind

Ginseng (*Panax ginseng*): Beauty, energy, fertility, healing, lust, sexuality, wishes

Goldenrod (*Solidago altissima*): Divination, money

Grapefruit (*Citrus × paradisi*): Removal, renewal

Honey: Making things stick, money, prosperity, slowing things down

Horseradish (*Armoracia rusticana*): Banishment, protection against illness, purification, removal

Hyssop (*Hyssopus officinalis*): Cleansing, protection, purification

Ivy (*Hedera helix*): Binding, entangling evil, protection, trapping evil

Jalapeño (*Capsicum annuum*): Baneful magic, stopping gossip

Jasmine (*Jasminum officinale*): Love, money, prophetic dreams, prosperity work, wealth

Juniper (*Juniperus communis*): Love, protection, protection of love

Lavender (*Lavandula angustifolia*): Family, happiness, healing, home, love, mental focus, mental health healing, pain relief, peace, protection, stress relief, sweetening

Lemon (*Citrus* × *limon*): Cleansing, justice, removal, souring

Lemon Balm (*Melissa officinalis*): Healing, road opening

Lime (*Citrus* × *aurantiifolia*): Cleaning, cleansing, justice, removal, souring

Mace (*Myristica fragrans*): Banishment, protection, removal

Mandrake (*Mandragora officinarum*): Baneful magic, cursing, empowering witchcraft, fear, hedge walking, mental distress, nightmares, spirit work, underworld work

Maple (*Acer*): Attraction, good luck, prosperity, success

Marigold (*Calendula officinalis*): Employment, healing, luck, money, protecting money

Masterwort (*Astrantia major*): Domination, control, persuasion

Mugwort (*Artemisia vulgaris*): Divination, psychic development, spirit realms, spirituality, underworld work, working with the dead

Mullein (*Verbascum densiflorum*): Courage, divination, exorcism, love, protection

Mustard (*Brassica juncea*): Baneful magic, chaos, confusion, problems

Myrrh (*Commiphora myrrha*): Blessing, cleansing, meditation, protection, psychic abilities, sacred to Yahweh, spirituality

Nettle (*Urtica dioica*): Breaking baneful magic, protection, return to sender, reversal

Nutmeg (*Myristica fragrans*): Luck, money, prosperity

Orange (*Citrus × sinensis*): Luck, money, prosperity, success

Oregano (*Origanum vulgare*): Healing, life, vitality

Parsley (*Petroselinum crispum*): Spirit realms, underworld work, working with the dead

Passionflower (*Passiflora incarnata*): Friendship, love, lust, passion, relationships

Patchouli (*Pogostemon cablin*): Love, passion, romance, sex, sexuality

Peppermint (*Mentha × piperita*): Calm, healing, pain relief, peace, serenity, stress relief

Pine (*Pinus*): Cleansing, fertility, healing, hope, luck, money, prosperity, protection, removal, success

Plantain (*Plantago major*): Power, protection, strength

Poppy (*Papaver somniferum*): Altered states of consciousness, chaos, confusion

Raspberry (*Rubus idaeus* var. *strigosus*): Attracting luck

Rose (*Rosa*): Beauty, love, lust, relationships, romance

Pink Rose: Friendship, self-love

Rose Thorns: Protecting love

Yellow Rose: Friendship

Rosemary (*Salvia rosmarinus*): Block busting, family, household magic, opening the mind, peaceful mind, road opening

Rowan (*Sorbus aucuparia*): Protection, protection against baneful magic, protection against witchcraft

Sage (*Salvia officinalis*): Banishing, cleaning, protection against negativity, removal, spirituality

Saint-John's-Wort (*Hypericum perforatum*): Overcoming anxiety and depression, strength

Star Anise (*Illicium verum*): Divination, meditation, psychic abilities, psychic gifts, spiritual work

Sugar: Attraction, money, sweetening, wealth

Sunflower (*Helianthus annuus*): Growth, hope, light, love, money, prosperity, wealth

Tea Tree (*Melaleuca alternifolia*): Protection, reversal

Thyme (*Thymus vulgaris*): Luck, protection, psychic powers, underworld work

Valerian (*Valeriana officinalis*): Baneful magic, distressed sleep, fear, nightmares

Vervain (*Verbena hastata*): Divination, meditation, psychic abilities, psychic gifts, spiritual work

Wood Betony (*Pedicularis canadensis*): Protection, purification

Woodruff (*Galium odoratum*): Courage, power, strength

Wormwood (*Artemisia absinthium*): Calling spirits, divination, psychic development, psychic sight, underworld work

Yarrow (*Achillea millefolium*): Divination, psychic development, psychic sight, spirit work

Yellow Dock (*Rumex crispus*): Attracting customers, money, prosperity, success

CRYSTAL, STONE, MINERAL & OTHER CURIOS CORRESPONDENCES

Crystals, stones, and other curios are common tools in spellwork. This list covers the crystals, minerals, and other magical items that have been mentioned in the text. Some additional curios have been added for use in your work.

Aluminum Foil: Protection, reflection, reversal

Amber: Ancestors, the dead, luck, protection against evil, wealth

Amethyst: Healing, meditation, mental focus, psychic work

Aventurine: Attracting money, attracting sales

Carnelian: Desire, love, lust, sexuality

Citrine: Money, luck, prosperity, success

Diamond: Love, luck, marriage, money, spirituality, wealth

Emerald: Eyesight, exorcism, love, mental powers, money, protection

Fluorite: Divination, mental focus, psychic abilities, psychic development

Garnet: Healing, protection, strength

Goldstone: Luck, money, prosperity

Hematite: Grounding, protection, reflection, reversal

Howlite: Healing

Iron Pyrite/Fool's Gold: Good luck, money, success

Jadeite: Healing, longevity, love, money, prosperity, protection, wisdom

Jasper: Healing, protection, returning negativity

Jet: Anti-nightmare, divination, health, luck, protection

Labradorite: Happiness, peace, peace of mind, relaxation, tranquility

Lapis Lazuli: Communication, healing

Magnet: Attraction, removal, repelling

Malachite: Business success, love, peace, power, protection

Mirrors: Protection, reflection, reversal

Moonstone: Divination, love, moon goddesses, psychic abilities

Moss Agate: Fertility, gardening, happiness, long life, riches

Nails: Protection, repelling faeries, repelling negativity

Obsidian: Grounding, neutralizing energy, protection, removal

Quartz: Empowering other crystals, meditation, power boost, spirituality

Rose Quartz: Friendship, love, passion, self-love

Saltpeter: Causing impotence

Sea Salt: Absorption, blessing, cleansing, neutralization, protection

Skeleton Key: Block busting, opening, road opening, unlocking

Sodalite: Communication, healing

Thorns: Baneful magic, banishment, curses, curse/hex protection, protection

Tiger's-Eye: Luck, money, protection, protection of money

MAGICAL FORMULAS

Incenses and oils are common ingredients in magical work, as are powders, colognes, and other special liquids. The following recipes include those found in the main text. All of these formulas use dried herbs to increase their shelf life. Using fresh herbs or a heat-infused method cuts that shelf life down by half or more. Incenses and powders are best used within six months to a year, but they can effectively last up to three years. Liquids have different shelf lives depending on the base used. Oils last four to six months. Colognes and sprays with an alcohol or vegetable glycerin base can last one year. Water-based sprays last one to two weeks.

There are three main tools that you need to create these formulas: a mortar and pestle, a mixing bowl, and something to mix with. Once you have made your product, you will need to store it properly. Incenses and powders can be stored in old spice jars. Liquids will often need to be strained through cheesecloth before being put into two types of storage: mason jars for general storage and appropriately sized application bottles. Application bottles are typically either a dropper bottle or a spray bottle. Dropper bottles work best for oils, while sprays work well for colognes. Always remember to label your finished products.

Crafting Herbal Recipes

Making these materials is easy, and all the processes start with the same steps. Incenses and powders are ready to go into storage once the grinding and mixing is complete. Liquid formulas require a few more steps. Follow the instructions in this guide to craft the following formulas and make your own blends.

CREATING YOUR MIXTURES

Follow this basic guide to create everything from loose herbal incense and magical powders to sprays and oils. To empower the tools further, create them within the context of a formal ritual. The * illustrates which tools are for liquid recipes only.

MATERIALS

- Herbs for your incense or powder (Having 3 to 2 different herbs is ideal; no more than 7 should ever be used.)
- Liquid base (alcohol, glycerin, oil, etc.)*
- Mortar and pestle
- Spoon
- Mixing bowl
- 2 mason jars*
- Cheesecloth*
- Funnel*
- Appropriate storage container
- Pen and label sticker

WORKING

1. Use the mortar and pestle to grind the herbs one at a time. As you grind the herbs, state why they are being used.

2. Once ground, transfer each herb from the grinder to the small bowl. After each herb is added, use the spoon to stir the materials. While mixing, recite a chant, phrase, or mantra related to the work at hand three to five times.

3. Once the herbs are thoroughly mixed, hold your hands over the bowl and focus on the goal of the work. Hold on to any thoughts, images, or sensations related to the work at hand.

4. When you can no longer hold your focus, release all of the energy, directing it into the herbal mixture. If you are making an incense or powder,

transfer the materials to the storage container and skip to step 13. If you are working with a liquid, continue to step 5.

5. Transfer the herbal mixture to the mason jar.

6. Fill the jar with the appropriate liquid and seal the jar.

7. Shake the jar to mix the materials, thoroughly soaking them in the liquid. As you shake, recite the same words from step 2 three to five times.

8. Store the jar in a cool, dark place.

9. Once a day for the next 4 to 6 weeks, repeat steps 7 and 8.

10. After 4 to 6 weeks, unseal the jar. Place the cheesecloth over the mouth of the second mason jar and carefully pour the contents into it.

11. Once the liquid has been strained from the first jar, squeeze as much liquid out of the cheesecloth as you can. Dispose of the cheesecloth and herbs in the trash.

12. Transfer a small amount of the liquid to the spray or dropper bottle.

13. Label the container(s) and clean up. Store the container(s) in a dry location away from heat and light.

14. To use powders, sprinkle or add them to the spell as directed. Incenses can be burned or used as fillings. Oils, colognes, and other liquids can be used to anoint objects. They can also be worn like perfumes.

Incense Formulas

Craft and burn these incenses to add power to your spells and rituals.

Spirit Offering Incense

Use this simple incense as an offering for any spirit. It also cleanses, protects, and attracts spirits.

- ½ teaspoon (2.5 ml) angelica root (*Angelica archangelica*) (for attracting spirits, banishment, cleansing, removal)
- ½ teaspoon (2.5 ml) basil (*Ocimum basilicum*)(for attracting spirits, protection)
- ½ teaspoon (2.5 ml) frankincense (*Boswellia sacra*) (for cleansing, protection, psychic abilities, spirituality)
- ½ teaspoon (2.5 ml) mugwort (*Artemisia vulgaris*) (for spirituality, spirit work, psychic development, psychic senses)
- ½ teaspoon (2.5 ml) yarrow (*Achillea millefolium*) (for divination, psychic development, psychic sight, spirit work)

Protection Incense

Make and use this incense for any protection work.

- ½ teaspoon (2.5 ml) holy basil (*Ocimum basilicum*) (for attracting spirits, banishment, protection, removal)
- ½ teaspoon (2.5 ml) frankincense (*Boswellia sacra*) (for attracting spirits, banishment, exorcism, removal)
- ½ teaspoon (2.5 ml) mugwort (*Artemisia vulgaris*) (for attracting spirits, protection, spirituality)

Meditation Incense

Use this incense to aid in achieving light meditative states.

- ½ teaspoon (2.5 ml) frankincense (*Boswellia sacra*) (for altered states of consciousness, meditation, psychic abilities)
- ½ teaspoon (2.5 ml) myrrh (*Commiphora myrrha*) (for altered states of consciousness, meditation, psychic abilities)
- 1 pinch mugwort (*Artemisia vulgaris*) (for altered states of consciousness, meditation, psychic abilities)

Underworld Incense

Use this incense as an offering to the spirits of the dead.

- 1 tablespoon (15 ml) basil (*Ocimum basilicum*) (for ancestor work, underworld work)

- 1 tablespoon (15 ml) patchouli (*Pogostemon cablin*) (for ancestor work, underworld work)
- 1 tablespoon (15 ml) parsley (*Petroselinum crispum*) (for protection, purification, underworld work)
- ½ tablespoon (7.5 ml) rosemary (*Salvia rosmarinus*) (for cleansing, drawing the aid of spirits, protection)
- ½ tablespoon (7.5 ml) wormwood (*Artemisia absinthium*) (for underworld work)

Magical Powder Formulas

Dirt is a common ingredient in magical powders. Dirt with corresponding properties can be a substitute for herbs.

Wellness Boost Powder

Use this powder to boost healing magic.

- 1 tablespoon (15 ml) rosemary (*Salvia rosmarinus*) (for wellness)
- 1 tablespoon (15 ml) lavender (*Lavandula angustifolia*) (for healing, mind, spirituality, wellness)
- 1 tablespoon (15 ml) sage (*Salvia officinalis*) (for protection against negativity)
- 1 tablespoon (15 ml) oregano (*Origanum vulgare*) (for vitality)
- 1 tablespoon (15 ml) pine needles (*Pinus*) (for healing, health, protection against evil)

Fast-Money Powder

Use this powder in any spell or working when you need money quickly.

- ¼ cup (60 ml) sugar (for attraction)
- 2 tablespoons (30 ml) cinnamon (*Cinnamomum verum*) (for money)
- 2 tablespoons (30 ml) alfalfa (*Medicago sativa*) (for fast cash)
- 2 tablespoons (30 ml) cinquefoil (*Potentilla fruticosa*) (for fast cash)

Protect & Removal Powder

Use this powder to protect and remove forces from your life.

- 2 tablespoons (30 ml) cayenne powder (*Capsicum annuum*) (for banishing, fire, removal, speed)
- 2 tablespoons (30 ml) ground black peppercorn (*Piper nigrum*) (for banishing, protection, removal)
- 2 tablespoons (30 ml) nettle leaf (*Urtica dioica*) (Banishing, protection, removal)

Anointing Oils

Apply these oils to candles and tools for additional magical charges.

Anointing oils use a variety of natural oils as a base to carry the essence of any herbs or essential oils that it comes into contact with. These are known as carrier oils. Olive oil, canola oil, and plain vegetable oil are not suggested to be used as a base oil as they can go rancid quickly. Common carrier oils include sunflower oil, grapeseed oil, coconut oil, and jojoba oil. Nut oils can be used as a base but are not recommended due to potential severe allergic reactions.

Healing Anointing Oil
Use this general healing oil to boost any healing magic.
- ½ tablespoon (7.5 ml) lavender (*Lavandula angustifolia*) (for healing, peace)
- ½ tablespoon (7.5 ml) spearmint (*Mentha spicata*) (for healing)
- ½ tablespoon (7.5 ml) marigold (*Calendula officinalis*) (for healing)
- ½ tablespoon (7.5 ml) allheal (*Prunella vulgaris*) (for healing)
- 1 cup (250 ml) carrier oil

General Anointing Oil
Use this as an all-purpose oil.
- ½ tablespoon (7.5 ml) frankincense (*Boswellia sacra*) (for blessing, cleansing, protection)
- ½ tablespoon (7.5 ml) myrrh (*Commiphora myrrha*) (for blessing, cleansing, protection)
- ½ tablespoon (7.5 ml) basil (*Ocimum basilicum*) (for blessing, cleansing, protection)

- ½ tablespoon (7.5 ml) mugwort (*Artemisia vulgaris*) (for cleansing, empowerment, magic, witchcraft)
- ½ tablespoon (7.5 ml) lavender (*Lavandula angustifolia*) (for cleansing, healing, mental focus, protection)
- 1½ cups (375 ml) carrier oil

Holy Crown Protection Oil
Use to protect your crown and spirit from any baneful forces.

- 2 tablespoons (30 ml) ground angelica root (*Angelica archangelica*) (for protection, removal and to repel)
- 2 tablespoons (30 ml) ground wood betony (*Pedicularis canadensis*) (for purification, protection)
- 2 tablespoons (30 ml) ground clover (*Trifolium repens*) (for protection)
- 1 tablespoon (15 ml) ground elder berry or flower (*Sambucus nigra*) (for protection)
- 1 tablespoon (15 ml) ground mullein (*Verbascum densiflorum*) (for protection)
- 2½ cups (625 ml) carrier oil
- 5 to 10 drops tea tree essential oil (*Melaleuca alternifolia*) (for protection)

Cologne & Spray Formulas
The difference between an oil and any other liquid is the base. Colognes and sprays use alcohol or vegetable glycerin as a base.

Homemade Florida Water

Use this popular water as a cleansing tool. You can buy commercially available Florida water or make your own.

- 1 quart (950 ml) clear alcohol or vegetable glycerin
- 5 fresh rosemary sprigs (*Salvia rosmarinus*) (for cleansing, drawing the aid of spirits, protection)
- 2 tablespoons (30 ml) ground basil or 3 fresh basil sprigs (*Ocimum basilicum*) (for cleansing, removal)

Flower Cleanse & Protect Cologne

Use this cologne to protect yourself while out and about. It will protect you from both spiritual and mundane harm.

- 3 tablespoons (45 ml) dried rose petals or 3 fresh rosebuds (*Rosa*) (for protection)
- 2 tablespoons (30 ml) lavender (*Lavandula angustifolia*) (for cleansing, protection)
- ½ tablespoon (7.5 ml) cedar chips or bark (for cleansing, protection)
- ½ tablespoon (7.5 ml) marigold (for protection)
- ½ tablespoon (7.5 ml) rosemary (for cleansing, protection)
- 1 quart (950 ml) clear alcohol or vegetable glycerin

Carmelite Water

Use Carmelite water as you would Florida water. It is less known but just as potent. Originally made as a digestive aid, this tonic also provides powerful cleansing magic.

- 1 quart (950 ml) clear alcohol or vegetable glycerin
- ½ tablespoon (7.5 ml) lemon balm (*Melissa officinalis*) (for cleansing, removal)
- ½ tablespoon (7.5 ml) lavender (*Lavandula angustifolia*) (for protection, purification)
- ½ tablespoon (7.5 ml) peppermint (*Mentha × piperita*) (for cleansing, purification)
- 1 cinnamon stick (*Cinnamomum verum*) (for protection)
- Zest from 1 lemon (*Citrus × limon*) (for cleansing, protection, purification, reversal)
- Zest from 1 lime (*Citrus × aurantiifolia*) (for cleansing, protection, purification, reversal)

Citrus Cleansing Spray

Use this spray for cleansing on the go.

- 3 cups (700 ml) ethyl alcohol
- 1 tablespoon (15 ml) rosemary (*Salvia rosmarinus*) (for home, cleansing)
- 1 tablespoon (15 ml) pine needles (*Pinus*) (for cleansing, home, protection)
- Zest of 1 grapefruit (*Citrus × paradisi*) (for removal, renewal)
- Zest of 1 lemon (*Citrus × limon*) (for cleansing, purification)
- 2 tablespoons (30 ml) lemon balm (*Melissa officinalis*) (for cleansing)

CONCLUSION

The society we live in today often makes it hard to remember that magic can be found and worked anytime and anywhere. As witches and magical workers, it is important to remember that the energy and spirits worked with to create magic are always around us. We just need to take the time to see and acknowledge them.

It is often said that one who is truly adept at magic can work magic anywhere and anytime with only themselves and whatever they have at hand. The strongest magical tool we have is ourselves. Any other tool we use is there to add power and help us focus. Finding other magical tools for our spells comes easy once you start to look everywhere around you.

Remember that dirt is everywhere. With the techniques you have learned in this text, you are able to cast a spell anywhere using just the dirt under your feet. From the dirt in your home to beach sand, the power to craft magic is all around you. Go ahead and tap into this power; you will find your magic has more strength than before.

Working with dirt is not clean or pretty—you will get dirty and you will feel the earth in your hands—but it is effective. Between communicating with spirits and gathering the dirt, you will develop a connection to the earth that will empower you for years to come. Get out there and dig in. The power within the earth is yours. You just need to be willing to get dirty.

In this book, you have crafted the tools necessary to develop relationships with a variety of spirits, plants, and animals. Use these tools to grow your power, connection to the land, and spiritual awareness. The world is full of vibrant forces that can empower and enlighten us. All of that power lies in the earth under our feet.

Acknowledgments

I'd like to give a special thanks to my literary agent, Bill Gladstone, for his support in finding a publisher for this book and to Heather Greene and the staff at Llewellyn Worldwide. Without them, this book would still be just a dream.

I'd like to acknowledge Christian Day, Brian Cain, and the staff at Warlocks, Inc. for creating WitchCon Online, where I was able to teach a class that over time became this book. Thank you for all of the support and the opportunities you have given me.

APPENDIX I
Exercises, Rituals & Spells in Order of Appearance

Part I: The Basics

Dirt, Earth & the World around You

    Sensing the Energy of Place, 12

    Aligning Your Body & Energy with the Location, 15

    Communicate with the Spirit of Place, 18

    Make an Offering to a Land Spirit, 22

Gathering & Harvesting Dirt

    Gathering Dirt & Paying the Coin, 31

    A Ritual to Harvest Dirt, 32

Ethics, Magic & the Law
    Ethical Questions, 41

Part II: Spells & Magical Works

Foot Tracks
    Protection from a Distance Poppet, 46
    Neutralize Baneful Energy Spell, 48
    Protection on the Go Charm, 49
    Heal Thy Wounds Poppet Spell, 50
    Wellness Boost Powder Spell, 52
    Mental Health Aid Candle Spell, 54
    Sweeten Successful Money Candle Spell, 56
    Fast Cash Bowl Working, 58
    Luck Gain, 59
    True Love's Light Candle Spell, 61
    Partners & Lovers Spell, 63
    Good Vibes—A Happiness & Peace Spell, 66
    Deepen Friendship Sweetening Jar, 68
    Remove Problematic Coworker Powder Spell, 73
    Curse Thy Name Spell, 74
    Repel Good Luck Curse, 76

Animal Tracks
    Observe & Identify Wildlife, 81
    Connect with an Animal Spirit, 82
    Ant Obstacle-Buster Spell, 86
    Fire Ant Wall of Protection Charm, 88

Parental Protection Bear Charm, 91

Topple Obstacles Bear Spell, 93

Strength to Change & Adapt Oil, 95

Reflect Inner Beauty Outward Spell, 97

To Be Cunning in Sales Candle Spell, 99

Attract a Lucky Day Charm, 101

Horned God's Blessing, 103

Speed of the Deer Healing Candle Spell, 105

Bring Luck into the Home Spell, 107

Conception Aid Charm Bag, 109

Snake Binding Spell, 110

Strength for New Beginnings Spell, 112

Termite Slow & Steady Destruction Curse, 113

Termite Confusion Spell, 115

Werewolf Oil (Wolf Shape-Shifting Oil), 117

Wolf Fear & Intimidation Trap Box Charm, 121

Home & Work

Get to Know Your Home, 125

Creation of a Hearth & Home Altar, 128

Ritual to Tend to the Hearth & Home Altar, 131

Protect Your Home While Away Packet Spell, 133

Peaceful Home Powder, 134

Prosperous Home Packet Spell, 135

Heal a Friend Paper Poppet Spell, 137

Attract New Opportunities Charm, 139

Enhance Love Candle Spell, 141

Attract Coworkers Spell, 143

Prevent Negative Customer Review Spell, 145

Listen to Me Spell, 146

Natural Locations

Mountain Protection Charm, 151

Mountainside Clear Sight Enchantment, 152

To Create an Immovable Force Curse, 154

Release Frustrations Cleansing Spell, 156

Return to Sender Protection Spell, 157

Blast through Blocks Road-Opening Working, 159

Home Protection Charm, 161

Hedge-Walking Trance Charm, 162

To Cause Nightmares Hex, 165

Bring New Opportunities Charm, 168

River Dirt Crystal Cleansing Spell, 169

To Cause One to Be Bogged Down Hex, 171

Ocean Beach Poppet Cleanse Spell, 173

Attract Sales & Customers Tidal Spell, 174

Tidal Chaos Curse, 176

Hide & Protect Me Charm, 178

Swamp Underworld Portal Charm, 179

To Bring Fear & Horror Curse, 181

Strength to Pull thorough Spell, 183

I Need Cash Now Spell, 184

Bury the Past & Move On Healing Spell, 185

Businesses, Public Services & More

Call On Your God Blessing, 190

God's Healing Spell, 192

Promote Healing Packet Spell, 196

Protect against Illness Sachet, 197

Mental Health Distress Hex, 199

Attract Money Packet Spell, 201

Protect My Money Jar Spell, 202

Sweeten Loan Application Packet Spell, 203

Keep Abuse Away Powder, 205

Peaceful & Just Separation Working, 207

Study Aid Packet, 210

Obtain New Skills Talisman, 212

Attract Business Ball Charm, 215

Attract a Place of Employment Spell, 217

Stop & Protect against Gossip Sachet, 219

Protection against Unruly Customers Spell, 221

Social Spaces

Increase Sales Packet Charm, 224

Gain New Friends Powder, 226

Attract Dates Packet Spell, 228

Self-Love, Self-Esteem Boost Charm, 231

To Feel Sexy Powder, 233

Loose Lips, Hot Lips—A Stop Gossip Curse, 234

Relieve Sore Muscles Healing Poppet, 236

Bring Peace to Chaos Candle Spell, 238

Increase Luck Spray, 241

Simple Luck Charm, 243

Desire Dates Powder, 245

Attract a Romantic Relationship Spell, 248

Road to Recovery Candle Spell, 251

Crossroads

Birch Coin Repel & Protect Talisman, 257

Attract Employment Packet Spell, 259

Abundance & Prosperity Crystal Grid, 261

Luck Boost Charm Bag, 262

Crossroads Skeleton Key Talisman, 264

Crossroads Dirt Divination Working, 266

Enhance Psychic Gifts Powder Working, 269

Distance Crossroads Healing Poppet, 273

Crossroads Fertility Spell, 276

Depression Relief Packet, 278

Full of Love Candle Spell, 280

Lust for Me Now Charm Bag, 281

Crossroads Binding, 283

To Send Away Removal Spell, 285

Reap What You Sow Spell, 287

To Make Someone Lost Curse, 290

Cemeteries & Graveyards

Cleanse & Neutralize Bath, 297

Rowan Protection Sachet, 300

Gathering Cemetery Dirt, 30

Ancestor Skull Spirit Home Ritual, 305

To Bring in Romance Candle Spell, 308

Interview Courage Charm, 310

Healing Bowl Spell, 313

APPENDIX II
Exercises, Rituals & Spells by Intent

Ancestor Work

Ancestor Skull Spirit Home Ritual, 305

Crossroads Skeleton Key Talisman, 264

Gathering Cemetery Dirt, 303

Swamp Underworld Portal Charm, 179

Attraction

Attract Business Ball Charm, 215

Attract Coworkers Spell, 143

Attract Dates Packet Spell, 228

Attract Employment Packet Spell, 259

Attract a Lucky Day Charm, 101

Attract Money Packet Spell, 201

Attract New Opportunities Charm, 139

Attract a Place of Employment Spell, 217

Attract a Romantic Relationship Spell, 248

Attract Sales & Customers Tidal Spell, 174

Bring New Opportunities Charm, 168

Increase Luck Spray, 241

I Need Cash Now Spell, 184

Sweeten Loan Application Packet Spell, 203

Baneful Magic

Crossroads Binding, 283

Curse Thy Name Spell, 74

Loose Lips, Hot Lips—A Stop Gossip Curse, 234

Mental Health Distress Hex, 199

Remove Problematic Coworker Powder Spell, 73

Termite Slow & Steady Destruction Curse, 113

Termite Confusion Spell, 115

To Cause Nightmares Hex, 165

To Cause One to Be Bogged Down Hex, 171

To Create an Immovable Force Curse, 154

To Bring Fear & Horror Curse, 181

To Make Someone Lost Curse, 290

Reap What You Sow Spell, 287

Wolf Fear & Intimidation Trap Box Charm, 121

Banishment & Removal

Birch Coin Repel & Protect Talisman, 257

Remove Problematic Coworker Powder Spell, 73

To Send Away Removal Spell, 285

Beauty

Reflect Inner Beauty Outward Spell, 95

Self-Love, Self-Esteem Boost Charm, 231

To Feel Sexy Powder, 233

Binding

Crossroads Binding, 283

Loose Lips, Hot Lips—A Stop Gossip Curse, 234

Snake Binding Spell, 110

Blessings

Call On Your God Blessing, 190

Horned God's Blessing, 103

Block Busting

Ant Obstacle-Buster Spell, 86

Blast through Blocks Road-Opening Working, 159

Obtain New Skills Talisman, 212

Strength for New Beginnings Spell, 112

Topple Obstacles Bear Spell, 93

Cleansing

Cleanse & Neutralize Bath Spell, 297

Ocean Beach Poppet Cleanse Spell, 173

Release Frustrations Cleansing Spell, 156

River Dirt Crystal Cleansing Spell, 169

Cut & Clear

Bury the Past & Move On Healing Spell, 185

Peaceful & Just Separation Working, 207

To Send Away Removal Spell, 285

Dating

Attract Dates Packet Spell, 228

Desire Dates Powder, 245

Lust for Me Now Charm Bag, 281

Dealing with Customers

Attract Business Ball Charm, 215

Attract Sales & Customers Tidal Spell, 174

Increase Sales Packet Charm, 224

Protection against Unruly Customers Spell, 221

To Be Cunning in Sales Candle Spell, 99

Divination

Crossroads Dirt Divination Working, 266

Enhance Psychic Gifts Powder Working, 269

Mountainside Clear Sight Enchantment, 152

Employment

    Attract Employment Packet Spell, 259

    Attract a Place of Employment Spell, 217

    Interview Courage Charm, 310

Family

    Good Vibes—A Happiness & Peace Spell, 66

    Parental Protection Bear Charm, 91

    Peaceful Home Powder, 134

    Peaceful & Just Separation Working, 207

    Prosperous Home Packet Spell, 135

Fast Cash

    Attract Money Packet Spell, 201

    Fast Cash Bowl Working, 58

    I Need Cash Now Spell, 184

Fertility

    Conception Aid Charm Bag, 109

    Crossroads Fertility Spell, 276

Freezing & Stopping

    Crossroads Binding, 283

    Keep Abuse Away Powder, 205

    Loose Lips, Hot Lips—A Stop Gossip Curse, 234

    Protection against Unruly Customers Spell, 221

    Stop & Protect against Gossip Sachet, 219

Friends & Friendship

    Attract New Opportunities Charm, 139

    Deepen Friendship Sweetening Jar, 68

    Enhance Love Candle Spell, 141

    Gain New Friends Powder, 226

    Heal a Friend Paper Poppet Spell, 137

Healing

    Bury the Past & Move On Healing Spell, 185

    Depression Relief Packet, 278

    Distance Crossroads Healing Poppet, 273

    God's Healing Spell, 192

    Heal a Friend Paper Poppet Spell, 137

    Healing Bowl Spell, 313

    Heal Thy Wounds Poppet Spell, 50

    Mental Health Aid Candle Spell, 54

    Promote Healing Packet Spell, 196

    Relieve Sore Muscles Healing Poppet, 236

    Road to Recovery Candle Spell, 251

    Self-Love, Self-Esteem Boost Charm, 231

    Speed of the Deer Healing Candle Spell, 105

Health & Wellness

    Bring Peace to Chaos Candle Spell, 238

    Mental Health Aid Candle Spell, 54

    Promote Healing Packet Spell, 196

    Protect against Illness Sachet, 197

Relieve Sore Muscles Healing Poppet, 236

Self-Love, Self-Esteem Boost Charm, 231

Wellness Boost Powder Spell, 52

House & Home

Bring Luck into the Home Spell, 107

Hide & Protect Me Charm, 178

Home Protection Charm, 161

Peaceful Home Powder, 134

Prosperous Home Packet Spell, 135

Protect Your Home While Away Packet Spell, 133

Jobs & Work

Attract Business Ball Charm, 215

Attract Coworkers Spell, 143

Attract Employment Packet Spell, 259

Attract a Place of Employment Spell, 217

Attract Sales & Customers Tidal Spell, 174

Increase Sales Packet Charm, 224

Listen to Me Spell, 146

Protection against Unruly Customers Spell, 221

Justice

Keep Abuse Away Powder, 205

Loose Lips, Hot Lips—A Stop Gossip Curse, 234

Peaceful & Just Separation Working, 207

Reap What You Sow Spell, 288
Return to Sender Protection Spell, 157

Love, General
Deepen Friendship Sweetening Jar, 69
Enhance Love Candle Spell, 141
Full of Love Candle Spell, 281
Self-Love, Self-Esteem Boost Charm, 231

Love, Romantic
Attract Dates Packet Spell, 228
Attract a Romantic Relationship Spell, 248
Desire Dates Powder, 245
Enhance Love Candle Spell, 141
Lust for Me Now Charm Bag, 281
Partners & Lovers Spell, 63
To Bring in Romance Candle Spell, 308
True Love's Light Candle Spell, 61

Luck
Attract a Lucky Day Charm, 101
Bring Luck into the Home Spell, 107
Increase Luck Spray, 241
Luck Boost Charm Bag, 262
Luck Gain, 59
Repel Good Luck Curse, 76
Simple Luck Charm, 243

Mental Health

Bring Peace to Chaos Candle Spell, 238

Depression Relief Packet, 278

Mental Health Aid Candle Spell, 54

Mental Health Distress Hex, 199

Release Frustrations Cleansing Spell, 156

Road to Recovery Candle Spell, 251

Self-Love, Self-Esteem Boost Charm, 231

Miscellaneous

Ethical Questions, 41

Observe & Identify Wildlife, 81

Study Aid Packet, 210

Money

Abundance & Prosperity Crystal Grid, 261

Attract Money Packet Spell, 201

Attract Sales & Customers Tidal Spell, 174

Fast Cash Bowl Working, 58

Increase Sales Packet, 224

I Need Cash Now Spell, 184

Sweeten Loan Application Packet Spell, 203

Sweeten Successful Money Candle Spell, 56

Prosperous Home Packet Spell, 135

Protect My Money Jar Spell, 202

Neutralizing & Repelling Energy & Spirits

Cleanse & Neutralize Bath, 297

Neutralize Baneful Energy Spell, 48

To Send Away Removal Spell, 285

Prosperity

Abundance & Prosperity Crystal Grid, 261

Prosperous Home Packet Spell, 135

Protection

Birch Coin Repel & Protect Charm, 257

Cleanse & Neutralize Bath, 297

Fire Ant Wall of Protection Charm, 88

Hide & Protect Me Charm, 178

Home Protection Charm, 161

Keep Abuse Away Powder, 205

Mountain Protection Charm, 151

Neutralize Baneful Energy Spell, 48

Parental Protection Bear Charm, 91

Prevent Negative Customer Review Spell, 145

Protect against Illness Sachet, 197

Protection against Unruly Customers Spell, 221

Protection from a Distance Poppet, 46

Protection on the Go Charm, 49

Protect My Money Jar Spell, 202

Protect Your Home While Away Packet Spell, 133

Return to Sender Protection Spell, 157

Rowan Protection Sachet, 300

Stop & Protect against Gossip Sachet, 219

Psychic Development & Psychic Gifts

Crossroads Dirt Divination Working, 266

Enhance Psychic Gifts Powder Working, 269

Mountainside Clear Sight Enchantment, 152

Relationships, All Kinds

Attract Dates Packet Spell, 228

Attract a Romantic Relationship Spell, 248

Deepen Friendship Sweetening Jar, 68

Desire Dates Powder, 245

Enhance Love Candle Spell, 141

Keep Abuse Away Powder, 205

Gain New Friends Powder, 226

Partners & Lovers Spell, 63

Peaceful Home Powder, 134

Peaceful & Just Separation Working, 207

True Love's Light Candle Spell, 61

Removal

Cleanse & Neutralize Bath, 297

Keep Abuse Away Powder, 205

Ocean Beach Poppet Cleanse Spell, 173

Remove Problematic Coworker Powder Spell, 73

River Dirt Crystal Cleansing Spell, 169

Reversal & Return to Sender

Birch Coin Repel & Protect Talisman, 257

Return to Sender Protection Spell, 157

Ritual Work

Ancestor Skull Spirit Home Ritual, 305

Call on Your God Blessing, 190

Creation of a Hearth & Home Altar, 128

Horned God's Blessing, 103

Make an Offering to a Land Spirit, 22

A Ritual to Harvest Dirt, 32

Ritual to Tend to the Hearth & Home Altar, 131

Road Opening

Attract New Opportunities Charm, 139

Blast through Blocks Road-Opening Working, 159

Bring New Opportunities Charm, 168

Obtain New Skills Talisman, 212

Strength for New Beginnings Spell, 112

Sales

Attract Business Ball Charm, 215

Attract Sales & Customers Tidal Spell, 174

Increase Sales Packet Charm, 224

To Be Cunning in Sales Candle Spell, 99

Spirit Work

Aligning Your Body & Energy with the Location, 15

Ancestor Skull Spirit Home Ritual, 305

Call on Your God Blessing, 190

Communicate with the Spirit of Place, 18

Connect with an Animal Spirit, 82

Creation of a Hearth & Home Altar, 128

Crossroads Skeleton Key Talisman, 264

Gathering Cemetery Dirt, 303

Gathering Dirt & Paying the Coin, 31

Get to Know Your Home, 125

God's Healing Spell, 192

Hedge-Walking Trance Charm, 162

Horned God's Blessing, 103

Make an Offering to a Land Spirit, 22

A Ritual to Harvest Dirt, 32

Sensing the Energy of Place, 12

Swamp Underworld Portal Charm, 179

Werewolf Oil (Wolf Shape-Shifting Oil), 117

Strength & Courage

Strength to Change & Adapt Oil, 95

Horned God's Blessing, 103

Interview Courage Charm, 310

Strength for New Beginnings Spell, 112

Strength to Pull through Spell, 183
Topple Obstacles Bear Spell, 93

Sweetening

Deepen Friendship Sweetening Jar, 68
Listen to Me Spell, 146
Sweeten Loan Application Packet Spell, 203
Sweeten Successful Money Candle Spell, 56
To Be Cunning in Sales Candle Spell, 99

Underworld Work

Crossroads Skeleton Key Talisman, 264
Hedge-Walking Trance Charm, 162
Swamp Underworld Portal Charm, 179
Werewolf Oil (Wolf Shape-Shifting Oil), 117

RECOMMENDED READING

Backwoods Shamanism: An Introduction to the American Folk-Magic of Hoodoo Conjure and Rootwork by Ray "Doctor Hawk" Hess

Backwoods Witchcraft: Conjure & Folk Magic from Appalachia by Jake Richards

Basic Magick: A Practical Guide by Phillip Cooper

The Big Book of Practical Spells: Everyday Magic that Works by Judika Illes

The Big Little Book of Magick: A Wiccan's Guide to Altars, Candles, Pendulums, and Healing Spells by D. J. Conway

Blackthorn's Botanical Magic: The Green Witch's Guide to Essential Oils for Spellcraft, Ritual, and Healing by Amy Blackthorn

The Book of English Magic by Philip Carr-Gomm and Richard Heygate

The Candle and the Crossroads: A Book of Appalachian Conjure and Southern Root Work by Orion Foxwood

The Casting of Spells: Creating a Magickal Life through the Words of True Will by Christopher Penczak

A Compendium of Herbal Magick by Paul Beyerl

The Complete Book of Incense, Oils & Brews by Scott Cunningham

Crossroads of Conjure: The Roots and Practices of Granny Magic, Hoodoo, Brujería, and Curanderismo by Katrina Rasbold

Cunningham's Encyclopedia of Crystal, Gem & Metal Magic by Scott Cunningham

Cunningham's Encyclopedia of Magical Herbs by Scott Cunningham

Cunningham's Magical Sampler: Collected Writings and Spells from the Renowned Wiccan Author by Scott Cunningham

Earth, Air, Fire & Water: More Techniques of Natural Magic by Scott Cunningham

Earth Power: Techniques of Natural Magic by Scott Cunningham

The Encyclopedia of 5,000 Spells by Judika Illes

Everyday Magic: Spells & Rituals for Modern Living by Dorothy Morrison

The Flame in the Cauldron: A Book of Old-Style Witchery by Orion Foxwood

Folk Witchcraft: A Guide to Lore, Land, and the Familiar Spirit for the Solitary Practitioner by Roger J. Horne

A Grimoire for Modern Cunning Folk: A Practical Guide to Witchcraft on the Crooked Path by Peter Paddon

Hoodoo Bible Magic: Sacred Secrets of Scriptural Sorcery by Miss Michaele and Professor Charles Porterfield

Hoodoo Herb and Root Magic: A Materia Magica of African-American Conjure by Catherine Yronwode

The Inner Temple of Witchcraft: Magick, Meditation, and Psychic Development by Christopher Penczak

Instant Magick: Ancient Wisdom, Modern Spellcraft by Christopher Penczak

Introduction to Southern Conjure (DVD) by Orion Foxwood

The Kybalion Hermetic Philosophy by The Three Initiates

The Little Book of Curses and Maledictions for Everyday Use by Dawn Rae Downton

Magical Herbalism: The Secret Craft of the Wise by Scott Cunningham

Recommended Reading

The Magical Power of the Saints: Evocations & Candle Rituals by Ray T. Malbrough

Magick in Theory and Practice by Aleister Crowley

Magic's in the Bag: Creating Spellbinding Gris Gris Bags & Sachets by Jude Bradley and Cheré Dastugue Coen

Magic When You Need It: 150 Spells You Can't Live Without by Judika Illes

The Master Book of Herbalism by Paul Beyerl

Old Style Conjure: Hoodoo, Rootwork & Folk Magic by Starr Casas

Papa Jim's Herbal Magic Workbook: How to Use Herbs for Magical Purposes, an A–Z Guide by Papa Jim

Practical Magic for Beginners: Techniques & Rituals to Focus Magical Energy by Brandy Williams

Practical Solitary Magic by Nancy B. Watson

Powers of the Psalms by Anna Riva

Rootwork: Using the Folk Magick of Black America for Love, Money, and Success by Tayannah Lee McQuillar

The Secret Keys of Conjure: Unlocking the Mysteries of American Folk Magic by Chas Bogan

Southern Cunning: Folkloric Witchcraft in the American South by Aaron Oberon

Spells and How They Work by Janet Farrar and Stewart Farrar

True Magick: A Beginner's Guide by Amber K

Utterly Wicked: Hexes, Curses, and Other Unsavory Notions by Dorothy Morrison

The Witch's Bag of Tricks: Personalize Your Magick & Kickstart Your Craft by Melanie Marquis

A Witch's World of Magick: Expanding Your Practice with Techniques & Traditions from Diverse Cultures by Melanie Marquis

The Witch and Wizard Training Guide by Sirona Knight

Working Conjure: A Guide to Hoodoo Folk Magic by Hoodoo Sen Moise

Working the Root, Vol. 1 of *The Conjure Workbook* by Star Casas

BIBLIOGRAPHY

Alvarado, Denise. *Witch Queens, Voodoo Spirits, and Hoodoo Saints: A Guide to Magical New Orleans*. Newburyport, MA: Weiser Books, 2022.

Artisson, Robin. *The Witching Way of the Hollow Hill*. Sunland, CA: Pendraig Publishing, 2006.

Casas, Starr. *The Conjure Workbook*. Vol. 1, *Working the Root*. Sunland, CA: Pendraig Publishing, 2013.

———. *Old Style Conjure: Hoodoo, Rootwork & Folk Magic*. Newburyport, MA: Weiser Books, 2017.

De Vries, Eric. *Hedge-Rider: Witches and the Underworld*. Sunland, CA: Pendraig Publishing, 2008.

"Deuteronomy 30:7—The Promise of Restoration." Bible Hub. biblehub.com/deuteronomy/30-7.htm.

Faerywolf, Storm. *The Witch's Name: Crafting Identities of Magical Power*. Woodbury, MN: Llewellyn Publications, 2022.

Foxwood, Orion. *The Candle and the Crossroads: A Book of Appalachian Conjure and Southern Root Work*. San Francisco: Weiser Books, 2012.

"Jeremiah 33:6 (New International Version)." BibleGateway. Accessed September 13, 2023. https://www .biblegateway.com/passage/?search=Jeremiah %2033%3A6&version=NIV.

"Matthew 6:9–13 (New International Version)." BibleGateway. Accessed May 26, 2023. https://www .biblegateway.com/passage/?search=Matthew %206%3A9-13&version=NIV.

McQuillar, Tayannah Lee. *Rootwork: Using the Folk Magick of Black America for Love, Money, and Success*. New York: Simon and Schuster, 2010.

Moise, Hoodoo Sen. *Working Conjure: A Guide to Hoodoo Folk Magic*. Newburyport, MA: Weiser Books, 2018.

Paddon, Peter. *A Grimoire for Modern Cunning Folk: A Practical Guide to Witchcraft on the Crooked Path*. Sunland, CA: Pendraig Publishing, 2010.

Penczak, Christopher. *The Inner Temple of Witchcraft: Magick, Meditation, and Psychic Development.* St. Paul, MN: Llewellyn Publications, 2002.

———. *Instant Magick: Ancient Wisdom, Modern Spellcraft.* Woodbury, MN: Llewellyn Publications, 2006.

"Psalm 6:2 (New International Version)." BibleGateway. Accessed September 13, 2023. https://www .biblegateway.com/passage/?search=Psalm %206%3A2&version=NIV.

Robbins, Shawn, and Charity Bedell. *The Good Witch's Guide: A Modern-Day Wiccapedia of Magickal Ingredients and Spells.* New York: Sterling Ethos, 2017.

"St. Peter." Catholic Online. Accessed May 9, 2023. https://www.catholic.org/prayers/prayer.php?p=186.

To Write to the Author

If you wish to contact the author or would like more information about this book, please write to the author in care of Llewellyn Worldwide Ltd. and we will forward your request. Both the author and publisher appreciate hearing from you and learning of your enjoyment of this book and how it has helped you. Llewellyn Worldwide Ltd. cannot guarantee that every letter written to the author can be answered, but all will be forwarded. Please write to:

Charity L. Bedell
⅍ Llewellyn Worldwide
2143 Wooddale Drive
Woodbury, MN 55125-2989

Please enclose a self-addressed stamped envelope for reply, or $1.00 to cover costs. If outside the U.S.A., enclose an international postal reply coupon.

Many of Llewellyn's authors have websites with additional information and resources. For more information, please visit our website at http://www.llewellyn.com.